HE HOLDS HER
HEART

Sara Eddard

ISBN 978-1-63844-374-2 (paperback)
ISBN 978-1-63844-375-9 (digital)

Christian Faith Publishing, Inc.
832 Park Avenue
Meadville, PA 16335
www.christianfaithpublishing.com

Printed in the United States of America

Dedicated to the Journey

For I am not ashamed of this Good News about Christ. It is the power of God at work, saving everyone who believes— the Jew first and also the Gentile. (Romans 1:16 NLT)

Have you ever sat down and just asked God
"What are you trying to teach me?" I did and
these are the lessons I learned. Ask God today
"What are you trying to teach me?"
See what happens. What's your first thought
immediately after asking this question?

CONTENTS

ACKNOWLEDGEMENTS

I dedicate this book to my mom and dad, who loved me through my darkest days and my best days. They've raised me on the word of the Lord and taught me the way I should go. Thank you, Lord. God gifted me with the best parents in the world. They encouraged me when I didn't believe in myself. They taught me to keep stepping, even when I didn't know where to step next. They encouraged me to seek the Lord in all areas of my life. I can't begin to tell you how amazing my parents are, outstanding doesn't cover it completely. They love me unconditionally and I am thankful and grateful for them.

To my big brother, Chris. My protector, my ambassador, best friend, and partner in crime (not actual crime, y'all). He's taught me many things and encouraged me through everything I've set my mind and body to accomplish. He's there when I need a shoulder to cry on, and he always finds a way to make me laugh. Seriously, the best big brother a girl could be gifted with. He doesn't see it that way, but I do!

My best friend, Susie. Oh what can I say, but thank you Jesus, for this amazing woman of God in my life? She is family even though she's not blood. She has been with me and my family through the valleys and just plain crazy. She's one of my biggest supporters, cheering me on. She encourages me right along with my family to take some of the biggest leaps of faith in my life. Thank you, Lord, for gifting me not just a best girlfriend, but for giving me a sister I never knew I could have!

My dear friend Sheri, thank you for always having a word of encouragement for me, always pointing me back to the Lord and his word, and praying for me and with me through the trying times. Thank you for never hesitating to share the wisdom God gave you, for correcting me with loving kindness, and always there when I need an ear to hear. I'm truly thankful and blessed with our friendship.

Most importantly, Jesus, because without him I wouldn't be the amazingly well-rounded woman I am. He changed my heart and my life over the years. He knows me better than I know myself and loves me in spite of the crazy I've gotten into over the years. He's picked me up out of some of the strangest situations I never saw coming and delivered me out of some interesting situations I got myself into. My life doesn't work without Jesus. I am blessed beyond what I can measure because of him. All I can say is, thank you, Lord Jesus. You have my whole heart and all of me, Lord!

These amazing people let me know on the daily how much I am loved, cherished, valued, and appreciated. I'm blessed beyond measure. I'm so grateful and thankful for my family. Moreover, I'm so in love with my Lord and Savior Jesus and the many amazing things he's done in and through my life. I'm truly blessed. What more can I say?

To the man, the stranger in the diner, who saw something in me and spoke it over me, I'm very thankful I met you that day. I only had the first chapter in my heart and mind, but you had God-vision that day you met me. You saw what God put in me and was about to pull out of me. Thank you for speaking His vision over my life. Thank you for speaking over me in faith that what you saw, God would bring to pass. I'm thankful I got to meet you before I ever began this process. That what God gave you to speak over me was over me, hovering, waiting for me to say "yes." I said "yes," sir, and here it is completed.

INTRODUCTION

1 Corinthians 13:13 NLT: There are three things that will endure—faith, hope, and love—and the greatest of these is love.

The most adventurous journey I've taken in my life has been with Jesus. This is my journey with Jesus and how he holds my heart completely. A journey of finding true love. A love unmatchable. A never-failing love. An unending love.

The Bible defines love as follows: "Love is patient and kind. Love is not jealous or boastful or proud or rude. Love does not demand its own way. Love is not irritable, and it keeps no record of when it has been wronged. It is never glad about injustice but rejoices whenever the truth wins out. Love never gives up, never loses faith, is always hopeful, and endures through every circumstance. Love will last forever" (1 Corinthians 13:4–8a). I feel like this is describing part of the massive character of Jesus in this scripture.

The dictionary defines love as "an intense feeling of deep affection." I feel like this is lacking in so many ways. Like love is just something minor, no frills, no muss, no fuss.

The one thing all humans crave is love. Love. Think about that, love. Love is more than a word; it is a state of being, not just a feeling. Love is the one thing we seek from the beginning of life. Love is the one thing we can never get enough of either. You search for it high and low, in all the nooks and crannies in your world, and in the right and wrong places. We have all done this. This is nothing new. We use people and things to give us the love we so desperately long for, yet we never find it in those places, things, and or people; and it never fully satisfies us.

You search for love and find it "lacking" because it's not the "right" love you have found. It's empty and hollow. The love you are looking for is only found in one place with one person, Jesus. He's the only one that can fill that void/hole in your life…more on that later.

Jesus gives you a love worth finding. A love worth seeking out in the pages of the Bible. A love that is pure and unadulterated, never-ending, never full of stipulations or conditions. Just honest-to-goodness love.

As you read this story of mine, you will see my evolution of falling in love with Jesus. A love I always looked for but never found in another person or thing, only in Jesus. His love is beyond words, beyond measure, and beyond anything we can imagine or comprehend.

He loves you right where you are. You can never earn his love. You can never make him love you more either. Jesus loves you the same today as he loved you yesterday, and the same will still be true tomorrow.

It is up to us to seek him, to find the love we are searching for, because it is only found in this one person, Jesus. It will not leave you empty or hollow. Nor will it ever leave you or forsake you. It rushes over and through you daily.

I hope my story helps you draw near to Jesus in a new and bolder way. If you don't know Jesus and want to, or you have questions, I hope this will help you have a revelation of his love for you and answer some of your questions. A revelation of his pure and unadulterated love he lavishes on you daily.

He loves you more than I have words to say to you.

John 3:16–18 KJV: For God so loved the world, that he gave his only begotten Son, that whosoever believeth in him should not perish, but have everlasting life. For God sent not his Son into the world to condemn the world; but that the world through him might be saved. He that believeth on him is not condemned: but he that believeth not is condemned already because he hath not believed in the name of the only begotten Son of God.

1 John 3:16 NLT: We know what real love is because Christ gave up his life for us. And so we also ought to give up our lives for our Christian brothers and sisters.

1 John 4:16–17a NLT: We know how much God loves us, and we have put our trust in him. God is love, and all who live in love live in God, and God lives in them. And as we live in God, our love grows more perfect.

CHAPTER ONE

Do You Really Love Me?

Ultimate Message: Jesus gave it his all because he truly loves us.

This is the story that Jesus said would change my life. He really did change my life with this little hidden gem in John. I always knew the story but didn't know the story in my heart. This journey was keen in my growth with the Lord. Without further ado, here goes everything!

> **John 4:1–30 NLT**
>
> Jesus learned that the Pharisees had heard, "Jesus is baptizing and making more disciples than John", though Jesus himself didn't baptize them his disciples did. So he left Judea to return to Galilee.
>
> He had to go through Samaria on the way. Eventually, he came to the Samaritan village of Sychar, near the parcel of ground that Jacob gave his son, Joseph. Jacob's well was there, and Jesus, tired from the long walk, sat wearily beside the well about noontime. Soon, a Samaritan woman came to draw water and Jesus said to her "Please give me a drink." He was alone at the time because his disciples had gone into the village to buy some food.

The woman was surprised, for Jews refuse to have anything to do with Samaritans. She said to Jesus, "You are a Jew and I am a Samaritan woman. Why are you asking me for a drink?"

Jesus replied, "If you only knew the gift God has for you and who I am, you would ask me and I would give you living water."

"But Sir, you don't have a rope or a bucket", she said, "and this is a very deep well. Where would you get this living water? And besides are you greater than our ancestor Jacob who gave us this well? How can you offer better water than he and his sons and his cattle enjoyed?"

Jesus replied, "People soon become thirsty again after drinking this water. But the water I give them takes away thirst altogether. It becomes a perpetual spring within them, giving them eternal life."

"Please Sir", the woman said, "Give me some of that water! Then I'll never be thirsty again and I won't have to come here to haul water."

"Go and get your husband," Jesus told her.

"I don't have a husband," the woman replied.

Jesus said, "You're right. You don't have a husband for you have had 5 husbands and you aren't even married to the man you're living with now."

"Sir," the woman said, "you must be a prophet. So tell me why is it that you Jews insist that Jerusalem is the only place of worship while we Samaritans claim it is here at Mount Gerizim, where our ancestors worshiped?"

Jesus replied "Believe me, the time is coming when it will no longer matter whether you worship the Father here or in Jerusalem. You Samaritans know so little about the one you worship while we Jews know all about him, for salvation comes through the Jews. But the time is coming and is already here when true worshipers will worship the Father in spirit and in truth. The Father is looking for anyone who will worship him that way. For God is Spirit so those who worship in spirit and in truth."

The woman said, "I know the Messiah will come the one who is called Christ. When he comes he will explain everything to us."

Then Jesus told her, "I am the Messiah."

"Just then his disciples came back. They were shocked to find him talking to a woman, but none of them had the nerve to ask, "What do you want with her?" or "Why are you talking to her?" The woman left her water jar beside the well and ran back to the village, telling everyone, "Come and see a man who told me everything I ever did! Could he possibly be the Messiah?" So the people came streaming from the village to see him.

That is the story of the Samaritan woman. Amazing, right?

Let me show you the way the Lord worked this story in me and ultimately changed my life. This happened in just about a minute in real life. When Jesus moves, he moves swiftly.

This is the modern version of the woman at the well. We are so self-fixated we believe we have to be completely together and perfect to be accepted by anyone, especially Jesus. However, Jesus teaches us otherwise in this story and so many others.

As she's walking to the well, she gets a glimpse of this dude sitting there, and I'm sure she's thinking to herself, *Oh, girl, did I brush my teeth? Did I put on my deodorant? Did I put on my new shoes? Oh, man, is my hair on point? How about those brows? Did I put on my lipstick? Oh, man, girl, he looks good!* She gets a little closer, and it changes the mindset. *Man, I bet he takes out the trash. Oh, I bet he won't complain about the meals I prepare. I bet he won't throw a fit if I'm five minutes past five with his dinner.* Even closer. *Girl, he fine! Woooo, he's so hot. Man, did you see that hair. Wow, long and flowy. Man and that tan, OOOOhhhh-laaa-laaa.* Internally fans her face. She's thinking, *I'm going to replace that guy at home with this one.*

All the while, Jesus is sitting at the well, excitedly, thinking, *Father, where is she? Father, I can't wait to talk with our beautiful daughter.* As she gets closer, his thoughts get better, *She doesn't even know how much I love her. Do you see her, Dad, oh, isn't she just so beautiful? Oh, I can't wait to tell her about the love I have to offer her and the life I have to give her.* All the while, they are both growing in expectation of one another. (Yes, I think Jesus gushes over us like that and in more ways than we can fathom.)

She is captivated by Jesus. She can't take her eyes off him. She knows there is something totally different about this man. She's drawn to him and can't even take care of her chore of drawing water because she is focused on him. It was something about those eyes, and that face, and his spirit calling to her on a deeper level than ever before. She knew. She just knew. He spoke with truth and knowledge. He being a Jew showed he didn't get his knowledge from the town gossip, and they didn't congregate together until after Jesus came.

> **"Have you ever been so captivated by someone and you just know you have to find out more about them? Something just keeps drawing you to them. That's what it was for me with Jesus."**
> **I am captivated by Jesus. I crave his word and his presence. I can't get enough of him. Being captivated by Jesus is invisible. You can't see it, but you can feel it. It's your spirit responding**

to its creator. That's why you're drawn to him. Your spirit says, "I've got to see my creator. I've got to commune with him." Your spirit knows that's where it's fed, recharged, and refueled. Your spirit says, "Hey, I got to hit up the well, Jesus, and get a new thing going on in here." The well is Jesus and your Bible is how you reach him. The Lord gave us sixty-six books and a boatload of pages to get refueled, recharged, refreshed, and renewed. Jesus says, "I am the way, the truth, and the life" (John 14:16). He also says, "I came so they may have life and life abundantly" (John 10:10). I stand and just openly receive his love. Fill me up with your love, Lord, because I know when I'm walking in your love, I will be more loving, caring, compassionate, passionate, kind-hearted, wiser, tougher, stronger, bolder, and more courageous because you reside in me. Greater is he that is in me than he who is in the world (1 John 4:4). With God all things are possible (Matthew 19:26). I can do all things through Christ who strengthens me (Philippians 4:13). I'm an overcomer in Christ Jesus (John 16:33). I am more than a conqueror in Christ Jesus (Romans 8:37). I am victorious in Christ Jesus (Romans 8:37). If I'm overflowing in his love, wisdom, knowledge, and understanding, nothing can stop me from doing what I have been put here to do.

We know she's captivated by Jesus at this point. She then has the understanding that he loves her. He didn't condemn her about her past. He didn't thrust shame or guilt on to her. He spoke to her with love, and it resonated in her and through her so much that she ran to tell everyone she knew. She couldn't wait to tell them of Jesus and his love.

I realized that in that moment, Jesus risked it all to meet her right where she was. A lot of bad things could have happened to Jesus for talking with her like that. It was deemed inappropriate for men and women to speak like that and not be married. Let's just say it was taboo—very, very taboo.

Then they have the most important conversation of her life at that well. Can we agree that she got a little bent when he asked her for a drink and a little defensive when he knew about her past? She had her socks knocked off, and she more than likely wasn't wearing any socks. She knew in her heart that this guy was for real. She was probably thinking, *Man, I have never had some guy I don't know offer to change my life before and make it so superior to what it currently is.* That's what I am guessing she felt for a moment, and when he said, "I am the Messiah." Wow! Talk about confirming what she was feeling in her spirit by the end of this conversation.

This story changed my life. It was the story God used to spark an even bigger fire in my heart for *him*. It showed me how much he truly loves me. I never completely understood Paul in Ephesians 3:17–19 when he wrote "And I pray that Christ will be more and more at home in your hearts as you trust in him. May your roots grow down deep into the soil of God's marvelous love. And may you have the power to understand as all God's people should how wide, how long, how high, and how deep his love really is. May you experience the Love of Christ though it's so great you will never fully understand it. Then you will be filled with the fullness of life and power that comes from God," until that day, when God showed me this story out of the Bible the way he did. I always knew he loved me in my head, but not fully in my heart. I always wanted to understand that scripture, but I didn't get it. That's the day I knew without a doubt Jesus loved me more than I could fathom. He moved the word in my head the thirteen inches to my heart! He touched my heart that day in a way that changed me even more than before. He taught me in that moment true unadulterated love. Love that only he truly can give.

That's the day Jesus began changing my ways of doing things and the way I see people. The day he began changing my mindsets and breaking things off me I was never meant to carry in the first place. That's the day I knew I was in it for the long haul. My actual words were, and I quote, "I'm in like sin." Funny, right? Totally inappropriate, or is it? Either way, Jesus has a heart for sinners, so it actually makes sense, or maybe just to me and my thought process. I don't know, but I thank the Lord he totally gets me! He knows me better than I know myself. That's why I always talk to myself, but really, I'm talking to the Lord because I need expert guidance, and who else has that but the Lord, really?

You know when you're trying to be that tree by the living water, and you go through a season—or seven—of growing (Psalms 1:3)? You're praying and seeking the Lord and then you get the breakthrough and it's like you got bigger? Well, you did. You got a little bit stronger. A little bit tougher. A little bit more bold and courageous. A little bit wiser. You grew with the Lord. That was me that day, but my love meter grew exponentially. This moment with God grew me and made me more bold and courageous, stronger, tougher, and— more importantly—loving and caring for my fellow man. God gave me his eyes to see people, his heart, and his love. I had the revelation of God's love that day. I finally had his understanding. Yeah, odd to say about love, right, but it's totally true. Solomon wrote in Proverbs 3:5–7, "Trust in the Lord with all your heart; do not depend on your own understanding. Seek his will in all you do and he will direct your path. Don't be impressed with your own wisdom." Yep, smacked me right in the heart with all kinds of feels and love! Thank you, Lord, for loving us so much. I said that all the time before and never completely meant it because I didn't have his understanding. Now I do, and no one—and I mean *no one*—can ever take that away from me.

That's what happens when the Lord gives you a revelation. The more you open your heart and soul to Jesus, the more revelations and impartations will flow into you from him. It's amazing to walk and do life with the Lord because he loves us so much and you see him in everything. You see exactly where to step or not to step next.

I used to think thoughts just happened or come out of nowhere, and that's just not always true. Sometimes, they occur in an unwanted or amusing fashion. Other times, they come to detour you or sideline you and slow your progress forward. Can I just tell you there are only two places outside thoughts come from—the Lord or the enemy. The way to truly know the difference is to know their character. The Bible tells us in Numbers 23:19, "God is not a man so he doesn't lie. He is not human so he doesn't change his mind. Has he ever spoken and failed to act? Has he ever promised and not carried it through?" The evil one is easy to tie down. The truth is not in him. The truth he cannot tell. When his lips are moving, he is lying. Whenever he speaks a lie, he speaks from his own nature, for he is a liar and the Father of lies (John 8:44). It's as simple as that. My pastor put it to me this way, "Did you feel guilt, shame, and condemnation? Or did you feel correction like your parents saying, hey, don't do that? And even easier, did it build your faith, or did it tear at your faith?" Knowing the character of a man shows you where they stand. It's the same with the Lord. He is for you. You know that going into any-thing. The Lord even had Paul write in Romans 8:31, "If God is for us who could ever be against us?" That means don't fear anything or anyone. *Nothing* at all. Humans can't cast you into outer darkness.

God's love is unconditional. We are the ones who put limits on God and conditions on ourselves and others. The Lord freely gives his love to every one of us. I dare you to say, "I love you, Jesus." I know as sure as I'm sitting here you will hear in your heart, "I love you, *place your name here!"* He is not shy about showing you his love. He will always tell you and, more and most importantly, show his love to you. He's not stingy with his love either. He doesn't withhold his love from you or me if we fall short, or fail, or make a mistake. No. No. That's a human thing, *not* a God thing.

I pray you open your heart to Jesus and allow him to pour his love into you and you grow with him every day of your life. I pray you get excited to do life with, and for, Jesus. I pray you always seek Jesus in all things. I pray you never stop doing what you were created to do for the Lord. Work gladly unto the Lord in all you do and be of good cheer and of great courage. Trust in the Lord with all your heart. He truly loves and cares for you in every way! Amen.

Reflection Questions:

1.   What or who are you captivated by today? Is it a speed-bump on your path or is it the Lord? What or who truly has your focus?
2.   Are you having trouble loving people? What does your love meter look like? Is it low or full?
3.   Do you truly know the character of God?

CHAPTER TWO

Who Knew?

You need to stay at the well at all times. You need that living water all day every day. You need Jesus every day and all day. You may not be happy all day, but it is a choice that is available to you. You may not be full of joy all day, but it is a choice that is available to you. We make choices every day, but why not make Jesus a choice every day? Why not talk to him and invite him into every aspect of your life? He cares for you. He loves you with an unfailing love. A love that never wavers. A love that never gives up. A love that doesn't keep count of when it was wronged. A love that never changes (1 Corinthians 13:4–7). We change because of the love of the Lord.

That's what happens. His love molds us into who he created us to be. It removes the crazy rocks and thorns we've stumbled into—or just plain ran into. When you know Jesus and you do life with him, sometimes you get off the path because of your own free will. I like to call it getting willy-nilly. When you get all willy-nilly, you pick up those things, and guess what? His love goes to work in us and changes and removes the dirt of this world.

That work is done through the Holy Spirit. Our comforter, our guide, our personal still small voice that says, "Hey, whatcha doin'?" (John 16:7) He waits for you to acknowledge Him. Usually, it's followed with, "Oh, you know, just playing in the rocks." He says, "Come on, little one, get back over here," just like your parents did when you were little.

He cares for you so much. He loves you deeper, bigger, and more than you can fathom or receive from any human on earth. How about that? Our Heavenly Father loves us so much we'll not understand it fully until we're with him in Heaven. Now that's a lot of love. A mind-blowing love. A love that just overwhelms me because I know what I've done, and yet he looks past our past and says, "Hey, it's okay. I still love you, and I've forgiven you. I've thrown it as far as the east is from the west" (Psalms 103:12). He chooses to remember it no more.

Stop allowing your past to keep you from your future. Your past has nothing, and I mean nothing, new to say. Your past doesn't define you. Your past is what got you to this point. The point where you realize that something has to be better than what you're living. It's your story, but really only a chapter or two of the whole story. That's the marvelous love of Jesus.

Jesus says, "Hey, that's just a blip in the book. I've got a plot twist for you, and you're going to love it. The story I'm writing for your life is great, grand, unimaginable, and serves a huge purpose. I'm going to blow your mind. I'm going to show you that your mess is a message that will touch lives, and I'm working through you to change hearts. Hearts that can only be changed because you had faith to take the first step. You were courageous enough to step out and let me, Jesus, into your heart." Your

Your story is only yours to tell. Only you know the path you have walked. Only you truly know what you have been through and what God has changed in your heart. You are brilliant and loved by your creator Jesus, and he will show you exactly where he needs you and which one of his children he needs you to speak to. He's sent me to some crazy places just to speak with his people that didn't even know him yet. It's okay to freak out. Trust me, I have, and I'm sure I will again. He's not surprised by us or what we face. Trust Him.

story will speak to many, and they will realize if Jesus did it for them, I know he will do it for me.

Your story will be the story God uses to touch hearts. He will use your story to remove that thorn or rock that's in the hard part of their heart and, oh, Jesus gets in. "Would you look at that?" Jesus says. "A soft spot. Now that's something I can work with!" Actually, he can work with it all and always does. Jesus really wants your heart and to do life with you. You were never meant to walk alone without him.

Jesus says in Matthew 11:28–30, "Come to me all of you who are weary and carry heavy burdens and I will give you rest. Take my yoke upon you. Let me teach you because I am humble and gentle and you will find rest for your souls. For my yoke is perfect and the burden I give you is light." Oh boy, does he ever give you rest, and it's the best kind. Wow, like you slept for two days straight, stayed fully hydrated, your arch nemesis "Pee" never showed up, and you wake up refreshed and renewed, but that happens every day when you truly yoke yourself with the Lord.

Troubles may come, but you rest in the Lord knowing he's fighting that battle for you, and guess what? You win because Jesus is always victorious. He overcame the world that day on the cross. Jesus said, "It is finished." That means exactly that, it is finished. What Jesus says he will do, he will do, in his time (Isaiah 46:11 and 60:22). Just so you know, his timing is so different than ours. Sometimes he says no, sometimes wait, and sometimes a straight-up yes. Yes, it's hard to wait, but it's worth every day to wait on the Lord. Jesus says, "Stand and see the salvation of the Lord" (2 Chronicles 20:17).

When I finally understood all of that, I hear the Lord telling me "he's got this and to trust him." In all honesty, I know it's Jesus' way of reaffirming me with that one sentence and letting me know, I'm his daughter, and he's got me. He's got my six. He has my life and my future in his hands. To trust him, he's got this covered, and I'm covered.

Don't worry about anything, instead pray about everything (Philippians 4:6). He's right. He's always right. He says in Matthew 6 not to worry, that he's providing for all your needs. He shows you in Matthew 6 your value and worth. He tells you how important you are to Him. He says, "You're far more important to me than the flowers or the birds." He's telling you, what I feel is, "Hey, I love you, I've got you, and you are so valuable to me that I'm taking care of it all."

Isaiah 45:2 NLT: I will go before you, and make the crooked places straight.

He sure does take care of it all. To the point where you look around and see nothing lacking, nothing missing, and nothing needed. He is your supply and your provider of all things (Genesis 22:14). Don't hesitate to ask him for your needs to be met. He tells us that many times in the Bible. He tells us to seek and ask our Heavenly Father for all things (Matthew 7:7–8, Matthew 21:21–22, and John 16:25–33). You have to trust that he will deliver what is best for you when the time is right, but more on that later.

You must understand that time is of the essence, and God knows that, but you must trust him to take care of the things you cannot see. Things that may be in your way to prevent the yes right now. Like I said, we'll talk about trust later on.

Reflection Questions

1. What choices are you making today? Are they self-centered or are they God-centered?
2. Are you sharing your story? Are you telling people how God showed up in your life? Are you bragging on God or are you taking the credit?

CHAPTER THREE

Do You Really Trust Me?

Has Jesus ever said this to you, "Do you trust me?" And your immediate response is yes, and then you examine yourself and find *Hhhhmmmm, maybe I don't*? This is what I know about trusting in the Lord. It is hard to get started because it requires faith and opening up completely to him.

I lived in a Jesus-sized closet for years. I didn't know how to navigate my walk with the Lord on the external, just the internal. I kept my mouth shut a great deal of the time about being a Christ follower. I didn't talk about the Lord until it was actually brought up in conversation, and then I only knew enough to confuse people more, at least that was how I felt. Maybe I didn't, but it was something the Lord used in me to open up more completely to him. It was the door I opened just enough for him to get his foot in. I say it like it was a fight—and believe me, it was. I was scared and fearful. I didn't want to open up to the Lord because of the fear of hurting more.

That's when I really started seeking the Lord and praying. My prayer went a little like this: "Lord, make me bold and fearless to speak about you and help me learn your word and understand your word. Lord, create in me a heart that's pure and on fire for you. Help me navigate what I feel and know on the inside of me to the external me, and help people see you in me. Father, I want to grow your Kingdom. I want you to say, 'Well done thou good and faithful servant.' I want to be pleasing to you, Lord, and not the people of this world. Lord, help me and teach me how to love and truly love my neighbors. Who are my neighbors? Teach me, Father. Teach me."

This, my friends, is the journey Jesus used to build in me a trust for him that cannot be matched by any human. I don't trust people the way I trust my Daddy Jesus. Yes, I call him Daddy because he says he is my Daddy in Heaven. I still call my dad Daddy too, so there's that.

Romans 8:15 NLT: So you have not received a spirit that makes you fearful slaves. Instead, you received God's Spirit when he adopted you as his own children. Now we call him "Abba, Father."

Trust is earned according to people, but God says to trust him in all things. Trust him with everything. He says, "Lay it at my feet, and I'll make it wonderful, but you'll have to wait." Are you okay in waiting? Waiting for the "already, but the not yet" is difficult. That's when your trust, patience, and faith are put to the test. In the "not yet," you experience the should-haves, could-haves, would-haves, and what-ifs in life, but you must remain faithful to the Lord. You have to block out all the should-haves, could-haves, would-haves, and what-ifs. That mindset has to be broken off you to get to the already, but the not yet. In those moments of waiting on the Lord, you learn a great deal with him and about yourself.

You learn to trust him and rely on him. I don't know what you're waiting on, but it will happen. The Lord says regularly throughout the Bible, "Trust in me," "This too shall pass," and "Thou shall not fear." These are promises from the Lord. Promises of him doing what he says he will do. Don't overthink it, and don't continually look back.

Philippians 3:12–14 NLT: I don't mean to say that I have already achieved these things or that I have already reached perfection! But, I keep working toward that day when I will finally be all that Christ Jesus saved me for and wants me to be. No, dear brothers and sisters, I am still not all I should be, but I am focusing all my energies on this one thing: forgetting the past and looking forward to what lies ahead, I strain to reach the end of the race and receive the prize for which God, through Christ Jesus, is calling us up to Heaven.

There is a reason that in a car, the rearview mirror is so small and the windshield is huge. Better to see what's coming at you than what you have already passed. The Lord knows everything you will face in life before it comes to you. He knows every good thing, storm, trial, and every sorrow, but with God, there is nothing to fear or worry about. He knows that this is going to make you ultimately better. Even the hard and sad moments will make you better, but don't allow these moments to make you bitter.

Stop worrying about everything that you may be facing and start activating your faith, trust, and patience. That situation will turn around. That need will be met. That spouse will come into your life. That job will be yours. That promotion has your name on it. That's what I'm trying to say. If God gave you a word—a promise, if you will—I want you to know it's coming to pass, but only in God's time. His timing is so different. That's why you go through storms or trials—to grow the areas within you to promote spiritual growth and a deeper relationship with God to help you in the waiting rooms of life.

2 Peter 3:8 KJV: But, beloved, be not ignorant of this one thing, that one day is with the Lord as a thousand years, and a thousand years as one day.

Sometimes God sits you down. He takes things or people away to grow that father/child relationship. You have to trust God. It's the only way it works that I have found for my life. If I'm not trusting in God, it falls apart at the drop of a hat, just saying. Jesus says he will never leave you or forsake you. He is at your right side. He holds you up in his righteous right hand.

Isaiah 41:10 KLV: Fear thou not; for I am with thee: be not dismayed; for I am thy God: I will strengthen thee; yea, I will help thee; yea, I will uphold thee with the right hand of my righteousness.

God sat me down for about five years. That's right, count them, five years. That's what I like to call my college years with Jesus. Certainly some growing, stretching, and trust exercises occurred for sure.

Oh, did I learn. I learned so much, I didn't even realize how much I learned. Silly me, I prayed and fasted to have a full and real tangible relationship with Jesus. Don't pray it if you don't mean it. If you ask, you shall receive. Seriously! I prayed that prayer for about six months, and then the Lord said something to me I didn't want to hear. He said, "Give two weeks' notice at your job." I said, "The devil is a liar!"

Guess what, within two weeks, I got sick, and it was terrible. I missed a week's worth of work. Got written up for missing a week's worth of work. Then I got mad. That day I cleared my desk and said I needed that stuff for my salon. I lied. That was a Wednesday. By Friday morning, I woke up at six in the morning, made coffee, and was watching Christian television to get ready for my day. Something felt off. I didn't feel right on the inside. I didn't know what or who or anything at that point. I turned off the TV and said, "Jesus what is this?" He said loud and clear, "Quit your job."

I fought with the Lord for an hour and a half. By seven-thirty that morning, I had texted my boss and quit my job. I felt a release in my spirit far greater than I have words to explain. I didn't ever want to do that to my boss. I really liked my boss. Since then, I have apologized to her and told her it wasn't anything to do with her. It was something I just had to do. I couldn't explain it to her because I didn't feel she would get it, which is probably wrong of me. How do you tell your former boss, "Hey, girl, I just fought with the Lord all morning, and he said to quit my job"? You know what I mean, not many people can fathom God doing something like that, but he did with me.

I felt so much release, relief, and peace in my spirit and my flesh. At that time, I was taking care of my mom. She was having quite a bit of heart trouble, so she had many visits to the doctor's office, pretty much weekly. With the Lord taking me out of work, it kept my dad at his job and kept him from missing days of work to take care of my mom. When I say it was a hard season, it truly was, but I'm so thankful for those seasons.

In my college years with Jesus, he gifted me with even more talents than I knew I could do. Like writing this book. Never saw that coming. More on that later. It all started with obedience to the Lord.

I've known Jesus my whole life. I gave him part of me at the ripe old age of twenty-one. I gave him my whole heart at thirty. You ask, "What?" It doesn't make sense. It will, give me time, and I'll explain it as best as I can. At twenty-one, I was born again. That day was a fight I'll never forget.

My parents and brother took me to a conference where Benny Hinn was speaking. God used that man to speak to my heart. I confessed with my mouth that Jesus was my Lord and Savior that day. I woke everyone up, including myself, at three in the morning with my hand in the air shouting, "I'm saved," immediately followed by me falling off the bed with a really loud thud. Concrete is hard. It was hilarious. We still laugh to this day over that night.

My college years with Jesus started in 2013, May 17, I believe. I'm thirty, going on thirty-one, in just a few weeks. Freaking out was an understatement. I said, "What am I going to do, Lord? I don't understand all this. I don't know what to do." The Lord, in true Jesus fashion, says, "Fast for three days and read my word." He told me this three times in one day. I knew it was him because when it is important, he will repeat himself, and the evil one would never ever tell you to read your Bible. Know the facts!

I knew the Lord meant what he said. He was answering a lifelong prayer that became serious a year prior. I didn't see what was coming until it happened. I got up the next day—a Monday, of course—and I had my Bible in hand. I prayed, "Lord, I don't know what to read in here, and I really need your help to understand your word. Lord, I want to learn and grow in you. Teach me, Lord, I think I'm ready." Right, like you ever truly know you're ready. HAHAHAHAHAHAHA.

I laugh at my prayer now, but Jesus didn't then. He took me seriously. He did what only he can, and could, do. He taught me his word, and along the journey, I fell in love with him.

He started me out in Ephesians. The great apostle Paul wrote Ephesians. He was smart, knowledgeable, and had God's understanding. I read that, and wow. Wow. I read that book many times that day. Took me forever to understand what the Lord was teaching me. It took off from there reading different books in the Bible and gaining God's knowledge, wisdom, and understanding.

My mom tells me that a few weeks into this life God was building and creating in me, "Do you realize your potty mouth has pretty much left you?"

I said, "No."

We continued talking, and I realized she was right. Aaahhhh. Something new. A breath of fresh air. I cursed worse than a sailor. Not joking or lying about that at all. By saying potty mouth, it's actually being polite, in my opinion.

A few more weeks go by, and Mom tells me, "Do you realize that you speak the word of God over and in every person you speak with everywhere you go?"

"No, Ma, I didn't know I was doing that." Another new thing God was pulling out of me.

Jesus had Paul write in 2 Corinthians 5:17, "This means that anyone who belongs to Christ has become a new person. The old life is gone; a new life has begun!" That's so true. The more time I spent with the Lord, the more things he pulled out of me that were bad and replaced them with his word and, more importantly, him and his character.

I finally understood the fruit of the spirit. I finally got it! Yay! I remember after having that conversation with my mom, and really examining my past few days of what I had said, I realized she was right. I hit my knees and began thanking the Lord for this new creation he was building, creating, and molding me into. I was so blown away at the power of Jesus.

Romans 12:2 NLT: Don't copy the behavior and customs of this world, but let God transform you into a new person by changing the way you think. Then you will learn to know God's will for you, which is good and pleasing and perfect.

I was blown away by how much he grew and changed me in a short amount of time. There were days I read my Bible nonstop for eight to twelve hours, stopping only to go to the bathroom or eat. I couldn't get enough of his word and Jesus himself.

Finally! Finally, I found what I had always longed and looked for. I found Jesus. Nothing, and in all seriousness, nothing, will fill the God-sized hole in you but God. It doesn't matter who you are or what you do, no amount of drugs, alcohol, sex, porn, food, money, things, or people can fill that void but Jesus. In my darkest days (that's what I call them because I was living for Sara and not the Lord), I smoked pot and drank like a fish.

When I met Jesus in 2003, I was delivered from those two addictions. Five years later, I climbed up on my big sassy "I don't need you, Jesus" horse and walked into a bar. Walking into that bar was a mistake. I got hammered. So stupid. I stayed in that pattern for a couple months. I got a nice awakening. Jesus gave me the biggest stupid slap of a lifetime—mind you, not the first nor the last time either. Jesus popped me on the butt and said, "HEY! NO, THIS IS UNACCEPTABLE. STOP IT NOW." I did it again the next summer too. I didn't learn my lesson the first time. That's how it goes. Thank you, Lord, for your forgiveness, mercy, and grace to walk this path with you!

I was falling into the wrong crowd. I wanted to be with my friends. What I didn't understand was that if I trusted God, he would bring me godly friends, and they would love and cherish me. If I had trusted God those two summers, I probably would have been a lot more productive, and they would have been less expensive. Those two summers taught me I am not stronger *than* Jesus, I am stronger *with* Jesus, and if I trust him, he will lead me where I need to be. He showed me to keep my eyes fixed on him and I can weather anything.

Micah 7:8 NASB: Though I fall I will rise; though I dwell in darkness, the Lord is a light for me.

He showed me in my college years with Him, "That I can do all things through Christ who strengthens me." As long as I'm looking to Jesus and trusting in Jesus, I can do anything. I can overcome anything. I can conquer anything, because I am his daughter, and he's already taken care of everything.

Now I don't try to do anything to fit in because I know I was born to stand out. I stopped drinking and really lost a great deal of friends. I know that sounds bad, but it's not meant to. I just could no longer surround my life with people who would bring me down instead of me helping to elevate them. Falling in love with Jesus taught me to love and respect myself and trust the Lord with everything. With Jesus, I know he's got my best interests at heart, and he tells me if I trust him and commit my way unto him, he will give me the desires of my heart (Psalms 37:4–5). Trusting Jesus was hard at first. As you can see from my past, I didn't always trust him, nor did I believe he knew what was best for me.

The day Jesus sat me down and began educating me, pouring his word into my heart and showing me true, pure, and unadulterated love, I realized I could trust him. I can trust that Jesus has me in the palms of his hands. I can trust that Jesus is my author and finisher (Hebrews 12:2). I can trust that Jesus knows where I'll be tomorrow. I can trust that Jesus really does have my best interests at heart. He knows everything I need to do. I trust him to provide a way for me to do that, and to teach me how to do it, and to get me and keep me safe while doing my assignments for him.

People destroy your trust regularly, so why not put your trust in Jesus, the one who won't hurt you but will care for you and love you through anything? Jesus is trustworthy. He has never failed me. He's never let me down. He cares for me more than I know or understand. I am so thankful I put my trust, life, all of me in his hands. I know he's never going to send me on a journey he hasn't already equipped me for.

This is Jesus at work within me. He's given me every word of this book. He is writing a story

> There was nothing wrong with my friends. It was me. I needed to change me. I was tired of seeing myself reflected back at me. I wasn't always the best me. I had flaws, and I still do. They are wonderful people, but I was jacked up. I needed fixing, correcting, mending, healing, and to be made whole. I needed to learn how to see myself the way God saw me in those moments. I needed to have his revelation and vision for my life. I needed to be with the Lord and break off my old lifestyle. I needed freedom that I knew not of. I stepped away from amazing people to become amazing myself, with God's help of course. I needed Jesus in a huge, massive way, and I found that quite quickly after a few years, of course.

through me to help you. I feel a little crazy for sharing that, but it's the truth. I trust the Lord to use this to speak to many hearts. I trust him to help me hold it together when people come against me. I trust him to have his will done in my life. I want Jesus to have his way and will for me. Sara only messes things up, but with God, I am far from a mess. I am a masterpiece (Ephesians 2:10). We all have trust issues, but I am here to tell you that Jesus can fix and build those trust issues into non-issues, and they will be superior trust bonds. It's up to us to place our mess, broken pieces, and ashes in the hands of Jesus. Jesus says he'll give you beauty for your ashes. He'll mend and heal your brokenness, and your mess will become a message (Psalms 34:18 and Isaiah 61:3).

My story is a story of Jesus' mercy and grace overflowing in me. It wasn't until I trusted the Lord that I saw his grace and mercy. It wasn't until I trusted him that I could understand forgiveness. I trust the Lord in all areas of my life. Trust is very important, and I will tell you Jesus will never destroy your trust. He'll mend, fix, and create it in you, but he'll never break your trust. That's a fact.

Reflection Questions

1. Are you holding on to the should-, could-, and would-haves, or are you fixing your eyes forward and on Jesus?
2. Are you trusting God with the thing, or are you holding on so tight to it, and trying to wrestle with God, so you can keep it to yourself because you think you know better?
3. What is he asking you to let go of? Is it a person, a job, a hobby, or a habit?
4. What have you placed on God's throne in your heart? Is God on the throne of your heart or is it another person, or social media, the news, what?
5. Do you really trust Jesus?

CHAPTER FOUR

What's Love Really Got to Do with It?

Love has everything to do with it. Walking in love is essential. "Love is never having to say you're sorry for what you've said or done" (typed in a sarcastic, very curt, and monotone tone). This quote is a fallacy, humanly speaking, but God doesn't apologize for your hurt feelings or if you are offended by his word or the truth. He uses every situation to grow and change us. When it comes to humans, however, we think we are entitled to an apology, but at the same time, we don't want to offer up or freely give forgiveness as freely as we receive apologies. I've learned through my many mistakes that I received more forgiveness, grace, and mercy when my apology is followed with changed behavior. God doesn't work that way. He expects you to change, but not without him or his help. Every day of your life, you are given a measure of mercy and grace because Jesus doesn't expect perfection from you, just right living, living by the word of the Lord Jesus Christ. He took your sin debt and replaced it with

> *Mercy* is when Jesus steps in and takes the bad that should hit you, and he takes the hit instead. *Grace* is when Jesus steps in and gives you something you should not be getting, also known as unmerited favor. *Righteousness* is uprightness before God. More on mercy and grace later.

a huge fat stack of righteousness (Proverbs 21:21, Isaiah 45:8, Psalms 85:13/111:3, Romans 5:8). Thank you, Jesus.

Jesus says, "If you abide in me, I, Jesus and my word also abides in you" (1 John 3:24 NLT and John 15:4 NKJV). Don't get me wrong, you need to apologize when you have said or done something wrong. Apologies mean a great deal, but changed behavior means even more.

We are held accountable for our actions by people and God. Knowing that you are loved, accepted, cherished, and cared for makes it easier to walk out your apology and change your behavior.

When you abide in Jesus and you seek him to help you change, it will happen, and it gets ugly and messy really quickly. Don't pray it if you don't mean it…seriously. If you aren't ready to change, you're going to fight, and fight hard. Change is necessary, actually essential, to grow with the Lord. You can't have a new you acting like the old you (Mark 2:22). It is not an order the Lord allows for long.

Knowing that you are loved and accepted by God helps you move through life. It helps you block out the hate and the nasty things people say about you. Yeah, you may hear them, but the longer you walk in God's love for you, the less it affects you because you already know where your love comes from, and that you are accepted by your Lord and Savior, Jesus Christ.

I love and truly love the ways the Lord works in my life. This story makes me laugh. I know I probably shouldn't laugh, but it totally hits my funny bone. I didn't understand this at the time, but as of today, I understand completely and clearly why it happened. Life experience always seems to outweigh what words I say.

Here's what I am talking about. A little example that really happened to me and I had forgotten about until the Lord put it in my head today. Funny! Lord, I love the way you work!

I was in the grocery store at the checkout. I had on jeans, a T-shirt, and hot pink Chucks. Nothing abnormal for my normal attire. Two young ladies got in line behind me. Cool, no big deal, that's normal. As I began placing my items on the belt and prepared to pay for my things, I heard this woman say, "She is unacceptable." I look around and realized they were talking about me. Awesome sauce. The kicker? They kept saying it with every move I made and every step I took. "Unacceptable." "She's unacceptable." "Unacceptable." Over, and over, and over. By about the tenth time of hearing how unacceptable I was in their "opinion," I was starting to get a little bent. I wanted to say something at this point, but what I was going to say was nothing nice or reaffirming. I was almost residing in a non-love atmosphere. My flesh suit wanted to unleash the fury. My spirit slapped it down. Nope, sorry, flesh suit, you aren't driving this ship. *You will bow before me flesh suit.* I just imagined Jesus saying that in my head with a very deep and rugged manly voice. Weird, I know, but hey, what are you going to do!

I paid the nice young man and collected my things and headed to the car. I immediately prayed for the ladies and asked God to forgive them for they knew not what they did. My spirit was in total control, and if not, I probably would have been in jail because of my flesh. I wanted to be mean, ugly, and hateful, but that's just not okay. I wanted to tell them, "Hey, sorry, I had plumbers crack, I just lost sixty pounds," but I didn't. When I saw them walking across the parking lot after I had prayed and already forgiven them, I wanted nothing more than to tell them about Jesus. I knew in my spirit that they couldn't accept that information, not right then, especially from this "unacceptable" girl.

That didn't linger in my mind. It didn't have time to take root in me because I am loved by Jesus. If this would have happened about five years ago, I would have unleashed the silver tongue on them, but I am thankful Jesus changed my heart and grew me. I don't have a criminal record, and I want to keep it that way. I don't ever want to be the permanent voice in someone's head telling them they are "unacceptable." Never again, in any way.

Proverbs 18:4 NLT: "A person's words can be life giving water; words of true wisdom are as refreshing as a bubbling brook. The name of the Lord is a strong fortress; the godly run to him and are safe."

Love got me in this, and love will always get me out. The essentials for change are prayer, reading your Bible, and seeking Jesus. In Matthew 7:7, Jesus says, "Keep on asking, and you will be given what you ask for. Keep on looking and you will find. Keep on knocking, and the door will be opened to you. For everyone who asks, receives. Everyone who seeks, finds. And the door will be opened to everyone who knocks."

When you seek God, he will show up and educate you, change you, and give you some much-needed insight and clarity. Everybody always says Jesus is love, but that's just a part of him. He's my ultimate protector, physician, provider, supplier, knowledge, wisdom, truth, and the list is endless really. I could write a million books about all of what Jesus is, but it doesn't matter because if you don't know him it wouldn't make much sense to you. You would laugh it off with a "whatever." Hear me, Jesus is far more than what we can comprehend on levels we know not of.

John 3:12 NKJV: If I told you earthly things and you do not believe, how will you believe if I tell you heavenly things?

Without God's character and love residing in me that night, I would have done something stupid and regrettable. My brother taught me a while ago you can't *un*-hear something. He's right. When I speak, I want it to be uplifting and life-giving, instead of spreading even more hate in an already evil world.

When I began learning how to control the smallest muscle in my body, the tongue, that was the day I made a change in my prayer life, a change that was essential for me. I couldn't keep walking around saying I loved Jesus and speak the way I was speaking. It has to change so that I can go where I am going. It has to be a difference maker. It has to not just act love but speak love over people, my family, and myself on the daily. It has to be changed, no ifs, ands, or buts.

Thank you, Jesus, for your mercy, grace, and love to walk this change out in my life every day. That was truly hard and something I have to maintain daily. It's not an easy fix, or a one-time fix, or an overnight fix. It's an everyday, all-day attention grabber for me, and I am by no means perfect at it at all. I fail on and off throughout my day, but I try to keep it on track the only way I know how…Jesus, of course, and lots and lots of prayer.

I once read in my Bible (1 Corinthians 16:14) and it says, "Whatever you do or say, say it with love." When I wanted to make this change, I prayed, "Lord, I want every word coming out of my mouth to be love. I want my tongue to glorify you, Lord." He reminded me of that scripture. It's stuck with me a great many years. When people ask me for advice, that's what I tell them, "Do whatever with love or say whatever with love. Just make sure it is done or said in love." I emphasize love all the time. When you are doing anything with love in your heart, and it is in the forefront of your mind, you are less likely to hurt someone's feelings or do something that enrages them. Offending them is totally different, and more on that later.

Everything we do or say should be done with love. Jesus tells us that many times. You get your butt so up in the air over something so minute that you don't even realize you forgot love about ten sentences ago. That becomes a time you may regret what you said or your actions. You can't take it back either. Wouldn't that be nice? A do-over button just to take back something mean and awful you said or did? That would be nice, Lord. That's the part that stinks the most. You can never get those words or actions back.

Once you have hurt someone you truly care for and you just made a mess, all you can do is apologize and receive forgiveness. If they won't speak to you, seek God in and on the matter, no matter what. He will always talk to you. You have to gain forgiveness for your part and extend forgiveness for the other parties involved. Occasionally, that is the beginning of the end of a relationship or friendship. It's part of life, and it will work itself out for your best interest.

Jesus tells us that the most unruly part of the body is our tongue. He wasn't joking, y'all. He was serious. I'm not going to portray that I have a perfect tongue. Oh, please, the Lord knows I need constant supervision with the matter, but you must seek God to get it in submission to him. Once you do that, the walk gets a little lighter. (See James 3:1–18 about control and Psalms 39:1–13 about not sinning with your tongue).

Remember that Jesus loves you. Jesus accepts you as you are. Jesus cares for every part of you inside and out. Jesus wants to make the essential changes in you. You know exactly what part that is, right at this moment. It could be your thought life, your inappropriate actions, and your lack of forgiveness for others that have wronged you, or the closet addiction you hide from everyone.

Guess what? Jesus already knows. It's not a secret. You think it is something he can't see, but sadly, you are mistaken. Jesus will help you correct and overcome it all. Your job is, in all honesty, to give it completely to him. In all seriousness, pray about it, and seriously pray about it all. He will guide you and take you by the hand, walk you through it, and help you knock down the walls surrounding you.

It will feel like you are falling apart, and you're a mess, and it's just not working, but I want you to trust the process he takes you on. I thought the same thing with all the essential changes I had to make. When you get on the other side of this, whatever it may be, you will be so grateful and thankful for all the Lord has done in, with, and through you.

You will be so elated to see the new you. The new shiny you! It will get scary and weird, and quite frankly, you will want to give up, but please, please, please, don't give up or give in. The people that love you will understand, and the people that don't get it, well, just walk away from them. That sounds mean and hurtful, but in all honesty, the people that truly love you will see the changes occurring in you, and they will be encouraging you on this path. You may have to tell some people "buh-bye," but you have to know and do the best for you, and you will know exactly what that is for you. Again, trust the process!

This might help you because it resonates in me pretty much daily. "The people that mind don't matter, and the people that matter don't mind." I learned this the hard way. Seems like I learn a lot the hard way. Hmm…(Sarcastically rubs chin with a naughty smile, all in a joking manner, and all seriousness hidden in laughter.)

When I truly started living for Jesus, I noticed a lot of people I thought truly loved me didn't really. They just wanted to hang out with the drunk or high Sara with all her inappropriate jokes and stories. They minded what I was doing and didn't care too much for the changes the Lord was doing inside of me, so it appeared. That's okay with me. I still love them, and I forgave them long ago because I wanted my God-given birthright as a Child of the King.

I wanted my eternity locked down with Jesus. I wanted to know true, pure, unadulterated love. I wanted to know why I was put here and what I was created for. I wanted a relationship with my creator, Jesus! I have many more birthrights just as you all do, but these are the ones I wanted most that the Lord used to start a work in me.

Don't freak out when you have to escort someone out of your life. It's all good, but do it with love. From time to time, season to season, you will have to escort people out of your life, so make sure you learn it the easy way and always, always, always do it with love.

How do you escort people out of your life with love? Usually, in my case, Jesus has truly done the escorting. I tell them I love them and that I am walking through some new doors. Which is true and the easiest way I have found. If they want an explanation, you are not required to give one. In the past, the Lord created a rift between the other person and me and caused us to just walk away from one another. It's okay to break up a friendship. It's just so necessary. Necessary for your peace of mind and heart. Remember, kid, it's all good. I know I say that all the time, but it's so true. It really isn't something worth worrying about because worry steals your peace. We love our friends, but doing the hard thing, breaking that friendship up, is the right thing to do for your life. Just because it's right doesn't mean it's easy.

Isaiah 26:3–4 NLT: "You will keep in perfect peace all who trust in you, whose thoughts are fixed on you! Trust in the Lord always, for the Lord God is the eternal rock."

Not everyone can go where you are going, and not everyone is privy to your walk with Jesus. They haven't really earned that knowledge. Remember that, *they haven't earned that knowledge.* That's something my pastor taught me. That's private information, and when God wants you to tell it, you will know when to speak up. You will feel it all on the inside. It feels like someone is standing behind you, hitting you on the back to get you to cough up that noodle you swallowed wrong, and it will usually just come falling out of you. At least that's how the Lord works with me.

Making essential characteristic changes are the most important changes you'll ever make with Jesus. These are the things you have struggled with throughout life, and it's time to put your foot down and make a change.

Seek Jesus to make your changes. It's the only way you will find with lasting effects. Remember that walk is long and hard and never the easiest road to walk, but extend mercy, grace, and love to others as best as you can while on your journey. (I say that because there were times I said and did things I am not proud of in my seasons of growth. Spiritual growth like this can get uglier than you can imagine, and more on that later.) Extend those same loving kindnesses to yourself. Learn to love yourself through all of this. You are growing and learning new things, and you have to fall in love with the amazing person you are becoming in the process.

I love you, and every part of you says Jesus!

Reflection Questions

1. What essential changes is God asking of you?
2. What's your prayer life look like? Do you have a constant line of communication going on with the Holy Spirit?
3. Are you giving out forgiveness? Are you extending people mercy and grace as freely as God gives it to you? Are you doling out forgiveness and extending yourself mercy and grace too?
4. Are you giving it all to God? That hidden secret especially?
5. Are you giving yourself or pieces of yourself away to people who have not earned that knowledge? Are you guarding your heart?

CHAPTER FIVE

What Do You Do When Life Hands You Lemons?

Storms and trials come, and it's mandatory. Mandatory, you say? Mandatory. They incite change, growth, spiritual maturity, physical maturity, mindset changes, and your outlook on life and your perspective. More on perspectives later.

The storms come, and you can't always pray them away no matter how much you want to pray them away. God doesn't work like that, but he uses them in specific ways to make the necessary changes we need. When the storms come, it usually challenges everything you know to be true and even your relationship with Jesus. No matter what may come your way, you belong to Jesus. You have to remember that you were blood bought and paid for in full by Jesus Christ. No ifs, ands, or buts. Ephesians 2:13 says, "But now you belong to Christ Jesus. Though you once were far away from God, now you have been brought near to him because of the blood of Christ."

If Jesus gave you a promise, more than likely, a storm or trial will follow. That's how it has always been in my life. It will blindside you, and other times you can see it building in the far-off distance. Who knows exactly why or how except for the Lord, and that's just what happens.

Always remember that Jesus walks through everything with you and that you are never alone. You may feel alone, but you are by no means ever alone. Jesus resides in you when you ask him into your heart. He knows everything before he allows it to touch you. It doesn't surprise him.

Just like Jesus, before he had to endure the most awful death for us, he prayed in Matthew 26:39, "My Father! If it is possible let this cup of suffering be taken away from me. Yet I want your will, not mine." He prayed that the Father's will be done and not his own. Jesus knows what is best for us. It is our job to seek the Lord and his will for our lives.

Matthew 6:33 KJV: But seek first the Kingdom of God and his righteousness; and all these things shall be added unto you.

Matthew 7:7 KJV: Keep on asking and you will be given what you ask for. Keep on looking and you will find. Keep on knocking and the door will be opened. For everyone who asks, receives. Everyone who seeks, finds. And the door is opened to everyone who knocks.

Matthew 7:24–27 KJV: Anyone who listens to my teaching and obeys me is wise, like a person who builds a house on a solid rock. Though the rain comes in torrents and the floodwaters rise and the winds beat against that house, it won't collapse, because it is built on rock. But anyone who hears my teaching and ignores it is foolish, like a person who builds a house on sand. When the rains and floods come and the winds beat against that house, it will fall with a mighty crash.

I know I quote these scriptures—well, at least the first two—quite a bit, but they are foundational in my personal walk with Jesus. They help me stay humble and help me fix my eyes on the Lord. They are a stable rock. Jesus tells us to have a sound and sturdy foundation in him so when the storms come, we will withstand the wind and the rain.

It doesn't feel like you are withstanding the forces of nature, but you are; trust me, you are. It feels like you are cracking under pressure. That's okay, it happens, and Jesus knows we aren't perfect. Jesus never expected us to be perfect. Look at Adam and Eve in Genesis. They failed, and they walked with the Lord in person every day until they didn't.

What I am trying to say is don't think you have to be perfect, because that sets you up for even more failure than you already experience in life. The process is long and hard, but you have to trust your creator to get you through the junk and the storms. The only way you come out of a storm with growth and transformation is walking through it all with the Lord.

I don't know how to describe what all that looks like, but I trust the Lord. Standing on his word and promises is what it looks like. When you hear the Holy Spirit speaking inside of you, you have a guarantee that it will be done. You know that because you already know the character of God.

Since you know God's character, you know he doesn't lie or change his mind. You know if

> Let me explain God, Jesus, and the Holy Spirit and how they are three but one. Think about an apple pie. You have bottom crust, apple filling, and top crust. Three, but it makes one pie. This is the only way the three in one makes complete sense to me.

Jesus said it, so it is. Simple as that, until doubt creeps in or worry or your past, but you have to tell those things they have no hold over you. Jesus is far superior than any worry, doubt, past mistakes, or failures. Jesus says that if you have faith to speak to that mountain to move, it will but you must not waver in your faith (Matthew 17:20).

We learned that this too shall pass (Deuteronomy 11:13–14). We learned that we are overcomers, more than conquerors, and in Jesus, we are victorious. Don't fear when that storm rages on, but rest in the Lord. He has you covered through all of the crazy that is surrounding you.

The storms will rage on to test us and our character. They show us exactly who we are and what we are made of. Our character is important. It shows what we

> We must align our faith with Jesus' faith because his faith is totally unwavering. I actually just learned this recently. When I align my faith to Jesus' faith, look out, I am unstoppable. We have already learned that with God, all things are possible and that I can do all things through Christ who strengthens me, so you and I become unstoppable.

can be trusted to do and what we can be entrusted with. Think about when someone entrusts their child to you to care for.

My best friend knows my character and entrusts me with her son quite regularly. She knows that while he is in my care, I will do my dead-level best to keep him safe, make sure he's fed, and that he is loved, just like her on some level. If she didn't know my character, do you really think she would give me permission to take him off all by myself? Heck, no. She would call me crazy. She knows I would keep harm from him as best as I can while I have him with me.

I remember the first time I took him all by myself. I was scared and worried something would happen, like a car wreck, or something even wilder, like someone would try to shoot up the place. He was fifteen at the time, and I voiced my concerns to him like he was an adult. He said, "Stop and let's pray," so we did just that. The day was perfect, we had fun, shopped and walked around, ate, I cut his hair, and politely returned him to his mother without anything happening. Every other time I have taken him, we just pray before we go, and we expect God to guide us and keep us safe. He always provides and never lets us down. Thank you, Jesus!

It's important to have Godly character. One, it shows where you stand, and two, people know you can be trusted. Trust and character go hand in hand. You usually can't have one without the other. Both are equally important in your walk through the storms.

It ultimately shows Jesus that you are unwavering. You will not be moved off the foundation he has built in you. That's a good thing. No wait, a great thing!

A solid foundation is the starting point in your relationship with the Lord. He, Jesus, is the creator of your foundation. It begins with being born again of the spirit, which is asking Jesus into your heart. Once that action takes place, Jesus goes to work. He works on you forever after that, molding you to be who he created you to be. He is a master craftsman. You can't build anything without a foundation. Foundation, foundation, foundation. Your foundation is what you should always lean on in times of trouble. As long as it is solid, so are you.

Zechariah 13:9 KJV: And I will bring the third part through the fire, and will refine them as silver is refined, and will try them as gold is tried: they shall call on my name, and I will hear them: I will say, It is my people: and they shall say, The Lord is my God.

No matter what life tries to throw at you, you can stand on solid ground, knowing you will make it through this, no ifs, ands, or buts. That's a promise the Lord gives us, and it runs concurrent in the Bible.

Ephesians 2:20 NLT: "We are his house, built on the foundation of the apostles and the prophets. And the cornerstone is Christ Jesus himself."

Foundation. We get this, yes? You know you can weather anything as long as you stand on the word of the Lord and his promises. It's not always easy, but it can be done. I myself have been there and done it many times. It's rocky, but worth every minute of every day of every month.

It's not just a "here today, gone tomorrow" storm. When you have a big promise you are pregnant with, the storm feels like it gets out of control and everything is falling apart, but it's going according to God's plan and serving a mighty purpose of purifying you and solidifying you. In order for God to birth that promise on the inside of you, you have to go to work on you. It's a hard road and really is the road less traveled. It's why so many people give up on their dreams and promises from the Lord, because it gets hard and taxing. You have to want it bad enough to fight what seems like tooth and nail to see it come to pass.

Isaiah 14:27 NLT: The Lord Almighty has spoken—who can change his plans? When his hand moves, who can stop him?

The first thing to get tested in the storm is your trust and character. Next to get pounced on is your joy, peace, and happiness. When your joy, happiness, and peace are getting kicked, just hang on and hang on for dear life. Let me tell you, the moment your peace gets kicked, you feel it down deep in your soul. You feel like you're a sinking ship, but you are far from a sinking ship. Don't abandon your post. Keep watch, for in a moment it will change.

Habakkuk 2:1 KJV: I will stand upon my watch, and set me upon the tower, and will watch to see what he will say unto me, and what I shall answer when I am reproved.

Trust in the Lord and know he's got you covered on all sides. There isn't a moment that you aren't covered by God. He has you wrapped up like a burrito, baby.

Don't allow depression to take root inside of you. It will try to drag you down even further than you can fathom. Depression will try to get you bitter, sad, and out of character. No. No. Tell depression to take a hike and just how big and powerful your Jesus really is. This is where you must speak the word of God out loud. If you speak it through tears, that's all right, but speak the word of God to that depression. Speak it until you believe it. Like the old adage "Fake it until you make it." You can't speak the word of God too long without it getting deep down in your heart, working and moving through you.

James 1:2–4 NLT: Dear brothers and sisters, whenever trouble comes your way, let it be an opportunity for joy. For when your faith is tested, your endurance has a chance to grow. So let it grow, for when your endurance is fully developed, you will be strong in character and ready for anything.

Psalms 118:24 NLT: This is the day the Lord has made. We will rejoice and be glad in it.

Psalms 54:4 NLT: But God is my helper. The Lord is the one who keeps me alive.

Scriptures like this help you combat the enemy voices trying to whisper in your ears. I'm serious, speak it out. Put your vocal cords to use, kid. Shout if you have to.

It never fails. When I'm in the shower or about to go to sleep, things like depression try to attack me, and I start shouting. Sometimes all you have is a whisper, and that's all right too, but don't ever be afraid to use your voice. If you have to shout or whisper praises, do it. If you have to yell scripture, do it. The enemy cannot reside in the presence of the word or praises of the Lord. God inhabits your praises. The light always wins!

It is written in James that if you resist the devil, he must flee. It's true. He does because Jesus put him in his place forever ago. Jesus is the almighty and all powerful. His name alone sends the evil one running as fast as it can away from you. I speak with truth and experience.

The current situation I'm in is coming to a rapid close, and I won't go into details, but I want you to know what I mean by experience. A few weeks back, in the middle of October 2016, I went to bed like any other Saturday night. I slept terribly, full of just awful dreams, and it had my spirit completely unsettled. My spirit was rising up in anger and rage. Anger in the spirit is a different feeling than what you feel when you are angry with someone. It's deeper and more vile than you can imagine. You feel it in your core almost down in your bones, and it's not something that you can just walk off. It's spiritual, and it has, and does, serve a purpose.

The dream I woke up from was a little girl that looked just like me, and sounded just like me, but it was a demon coming for me. Crazy, I know, but just wait, it gets better. I woke up, like I said, in a spiritual rage. I couldn't move nor speak, literally. I began praising the Lord in my head and screaming scripture in my head. I was being suffocated, literally. Not joking. I really didn't know how to handle this in my flesh, but I sure knew how to handle it in my spirit. I was a full-on rage machine. I resided at Defcon 1 in my anger level for a great deal of my life. Like I said, rage machine.

I was finally able to get myself out of my bed and walk down the hall to my parent's room. My mom was awake and saw a dark figure follow me in the room. I finally got my dad awake, and he got up with a start. I haven't seen my pop move that quickly in a long time. My dad began praying over me. He called this demon out and asked its name. Great! YAY (she says with jazz hands in a sarcastic tone)! Like you really want to ask what the creepy demon's name is? Actually, you do, so you and Jesus can handle your business.

It said, "I'm Satan, and I'm taking you with me" (I heard this in the depths of my soul). First thing out of my mouth was "The devil is a liar," followed by a few explicit words I won't repeat. (Case in point. See my tongue not in line here. Terrible curse words. Terrible). I was mad. Madder than a cat on a hot tin roof. I thought my flesh was a rage machine. Yeah, right, nothing like my spirit. My spirit was ready to kill and do damage. My dad began praying and quoting scripture, and the demon ran for the hill country. I could actually hear it screaming in agony as my pop spoke the word of God.

That's what I'm trying to tell you. With big promises from the Lord, you face big storms. We never know what is in those storm clouds. You don't know what will attack you or come at you at any given moment, so that's why it's important to have a solid foundation in the word of the Lord. Why it's important for you to keep your eyes fixed on Jesus. That is why a community of friends and/or family of believers is important. When your voice is stifled, you need someone to speak the word over you on your behalf.

I read my Bible daily, and I am always speaking with and consulting the Lord on everything in my life. That relationship is the most important and valuable relationship I have. Don't get me wrong, I love my family and friends more than you can imagine, but if I keep my relationship with Jesus ongoing and growing, I can cherish the ones I love even more.

I am not telling you that you will experience everything I have, but know that each person has their own path to walk with the Lord. I have no clue what you might be facing, but I do know that Jesus is right there with you, waiting for you to tag him into the ring.

I hope this story of mine did not scare you because it wasn't meant to. It was to inform you of the importance of keeping your focus on the Lord, because of his expert guidance needed in situations such as this. Jesus loves and cares for you so much, and I just encourage you to seek him in all areas of your life no matter what you walk through or experience.

I never thought in a million years that my purpose was so big that Satan himself would attack me. We have forces coming against us every day to try and stop or detour us from teaching others about Jesus and achieving our destiny and calling. The evil one doesn't want you to know how loved and cherished you are by Jesus. He wants you down in the dumps, broken, tattered, feeling like complete nothingness, and that you are worthless.

Jesus is the total opposite. He wants you to know that you are loved, cherished, irreplaceable, valuable, worthy, magnificent, and beautiful. Jesus calls you his child, friend, and his body and church. You are more than any storm or trial you walk through. You must know that you are worthy of everything Jesus calls you and tells you every day.

You are not a mistake, and you are in no way an accident. You were placed on this earth for such a time as this. You were fearfully and wonderfully made (Psalms 139:14). Jesus calls you the apple of his eye (Zechariah 2:8–9). Jesus calls you chosen (Matthew 22:14). Jesus set you apart for himself to do great and mighty things for the Kingdom of God (Psalms 4:3 and Philippians 2:13). Don't ever let your situation or storm tell you differently (Ephesians 1:3–6).

When life hands you lemons, and you don't know how to make that flavor of lemonade, seek Jesus, and he will teach you the proper recipe. Jesus will never hesitate to give you knowledge and understanding, even though it may come after the storm has passed. Just remember to hold on and stand firm on the word of the Lord.

Reflection Questions

1. What has the Lord promised you? Are you holding fast and true to God's word about those promises?
2. What scriptures built your foundation? How sturdy is your foundation? Are you reinforcing your foundation regularly?
3. Are your emotions attacking you? What are they speaking? Are you listening and seeking God to answer those emotions?
4. What lemons do you have? Have you asked Jesus for that flavor's recipe?

CHAPTER SIX

Who Knows, but God?

Galatians 6:9 NLT: And let us not lose heart and grow weary and faint in acting nobly and doing right, for in due time and at the appointed season we shall reap, if we do not loosen and relax our courage and faint.

Hebrews 11:1 KJV: Now faith is the substance of things hoped for, the evidence of things not seen.

Matthew 21:22 KJV: And whatever you ask for in prayer, having faith and believing, you will receive.

Luke 1:37 NLT: For with God nothing is ever impossible and no word from God shall be without power or impossible of fulfillment.

This is what I know about blessings thus far. They happen often, and they are powerful and heavy, like a magnificent weight has been laid on you. You know it is the Glory of the Lord resting upon you. It's far greater than you or I could ever fathom. The battle that got you this far is outweighed by the glory, favor, increase, and manifestation of the blessing of the Lord. Trust God in his timing, and you will not be disappointed.

This greatness truly is worth the effort, fight, prayer, fasting, and prayer. Seriously, prayer, y'all. It's a key right along with believing in the word of God. When you trust in Jesus this all happens, but you have to truly trust in Jesus. You cannot let doubt, worry, or fear give way to you quitting.

"Quitters never prosper" is a true statement. If you quit and give up on God before you reach your final destination, how could you possibly prosper? You cannot quit before you reach the next level. If you quit, then what was the purpose to begin with? Why start fighting the battle and not see it to the VICTORY! If you pray, remember Jesus will take you seriously, so don't pray it if you don't mean it or you are halfhearted about the outcome (James 1:5–6).

God is looking for someone to say yes to him. He wants to bless you so you can go on and bless others. It is more blessed to give than to receive (Acts 20:5). I know that scripture is truer than true. I have lived it for quite a few years now, and Jesus wasn't joking when he spoke it either.

Like I said, experience outweighs any words I could speak. If someone is telling you something from personal experience, you know they aren't pulling your leg about the results they received. They have factual evidence to back them up, and we see Jesus' factual evidence throughout the entire Bible. Everyone that gave was blessed even more. Whom much is given, much is required (Luke 12:48).

So much of you is changed while you are in the battle getting to your increase and blessings. That way you are equipped to walk into your increase. If God calls you, which he does call all of us, he will not let you wander aimlessly. God will equip you before he lets you operate in what he's called you to do for the Kingdom. God has a purpose for good, for everything we go through.

Matthew 22:14 NLT: For many are called, but few are chosen (Read 1–14 for the whole story about the Kingdom of God).

Being equipped by God is not always easy either. He pulls things out of you and replaces them with far greater gifts and talents than you can comprehend at the beginning. The *great news* is that Jesus is right there with you, walking out everything he's set for you to accomplish. Trust in Jesus and in his timing to work out all the things in your life. It takes time, but it is not something you want to rush through. Okay, yes you do, but know this, Jesus will slow you down to a snail's pace if you aren't learning what you need to be learning! When he sat me down five years ago, I didn't see all this unfolding, but I am grateful for this journey and adventure. I truly wouldn't trade it for the world, that's for sure.

I am so thankful for the lessons I've learned and been taught over this time. It's instilled so much change on the inside of me that I probably couldn't even list it all out for you without many hours with Jesus to write it all down. The journey is worth every moment no matter the difficulty, because that's when Jesus is molding us into who he created us to be. This makes me think of Romans 8:28, "And we know that God causes everything to work together for the good of those who love God." You know, I never understood this scripture until I lived it out in real time. God has a way of teaching you his word when you are in a place to receive it. Living that scripture is literally watching and seeing God's hand in everything that is involved in your life: the good, the bad, the downright ugly, and even all the majestic stuff too. Everything about you is important to God. Along this path it will be thrown in your face that God doesn't care for you because _____ (fill in the blank). He does care for you and more than we will ever know or understand this side of Heaven.

Let's get back to the weight of the blessings. It's a great weight, and the Lord your God is helping you carry said weight. He is right beside you, giving you expert guidance; you just have to be still to hear him. He's quiet for a reason. He wants your full undivided attention. He wants your complete focus on him.

The only way you can really and truly walk out all of the crazy seasons of life is with Jesus. I've tried to do it on my own, and I fail every time. I am thankful he's always correcting me and keeping me on track with him. He may let me stray, but it is never very long. I hear his promptings quite quickly now days. He helps me focus on him and his ways every day. It's magnificent that something I pray for, and to me, it's something so minute in the grand scheme of things, but he still answers my prayer because he cares for me. He is taking care of all my needs no matter how small or trivial or massive they may be. He's a good Father for sure!

The blessing is going to knock your socks off because it will be better, bigger, and greater than you can truly ask, think, or imagine (Ephesians 3:20). David says in Psalms 37:4, "Take delight in the

Lord, and he will give you your heart's desires." Think about that for a moment. Truly think about that for a moment. The desires of your heart. (If you want, take a minute to truly dwell on those desires you could even write them down. Put it out there bold where you can see it). He put those desires in you for such a time as this. Jesus did that when he created you. It's up to us to give him total creative control in our hearts. He knows what your purpose is. Your desires will line up with his word, your passion, your gifts, and your talents he's so kindly and neatly placed on the inside of you.

The scripture says he knew you before he formed you in your mother's womb (Jeremiah 1:5). He placed all these things on the inside of you way back when so that he could pull them out as you grow with him. How awesome! I mean, really, people, it's mind-blowing for me!

Your gifts get you in the room and it's your personality (character, morals, and ethics) that keep you in the room. When you are walking in your God-given blessings, favor, and your birthrights, they can't get away from you. They see them on you. They want what you have, and they want to see all of it. They want to know what they are seeing because they cannot comprehend all they are feeling, let alone what they are seeing on and over you. You do not have to share all that you know with people who do not deserve to know. Just be kind and loving when you tell them no. All you need to tell them is Jesus. They will be asking themselves, "How did you get to this meeting we don't even know you?" Your response should automatically be Jesus' favor, but you more than likely won't say that out loud. However, be honest with whoever it is you are speaking with in this situation. Most likely they will know on the inside exactly how you got to that position and placed before them, but let's be honest, they won't admit it. God's openings are profound and indescribable.

Jesus places you right where you need to be at the exact time you need to be there with the exact thing, word, or knowledge at the appropriate and perfect time. It's just another blessing Jesus is bestowing upon you. Jesus is the God of more, more than enough, overflowing in the more. He has a purpose for everything. Nothing is wasted or too small for him to use in your life to bless you and/or bless someone through you. Remember that or write it down if you have to, but house that in your memory bank!

Everything I have experienced in life has had a purpose, no matter how big or small, it all mattered and matters in the grand picture of my life story, just as it is in your life story. Nothing is a coincidence. Nothing is happenstance. It's all to bless, grow, teach, help, inform, transform, or change you in some way. The molding, if you will. In the gospels, it says that Jesus is the potter and we are the clay. It's all about relinquishing control to Jesus. Allowing Jesus to take over and form you into the human he's always created you to be. He's ever-growing and molding you for your good and Glory to God. He loves to show you all kinds of love, and you should be aware of that concept by now. Although it's not really a concept as it really is a matter of fact. Jesus loves you, and I love you!

I had this vision some time ago. What I saw was a yellow cab like the ones you see in New York City. I was in the back seat with my feet up on the back of the front seat, just chilling, watching out the window. I looked up at the driver, and it was without a doubt Jesus. When I realized it was him driving the cab, I sat up and listened intently. He was coming to a stop at a very busy corner in a city I have never seen before in real life or on television. He was giving me an assignment. I have no clue what that assignment was, but he stopped the cab, and we got out together at this intersection. Then the vision was over. I was allowing him to lead and guide me in this vision. When I came to, I told the Lord that's what I wanted. I wanted him to be my driving force. I wanted him to have complete control of where I am heading and how I will get there. I wanted to truly be submitted to the Lord. More on submission later.

It's hard to give up that control. It's so hard. It's like being that backseat driver no one can really stand…you just have to be the one in control or in charge. You get in your own way more than you care to admit. It's all right, we all do it, and Jesus has the answer to all those moments already lined up for us. Thank you, Jesus, for your grace! Give Jesus the controls because with him at the helm, you will get to where you are going much faster, safer, and in tune with him the whole way.

Psalms 37:23–24 NLT: The steps of the godly are directed by the Lord. He delights in every detail of their lives. Though they stumble, they will not fall, for the Lord holds them by the hand.

What a promise and a blessing knowing that Jesus will direct our paths for his Glory just lights my soul on fire for real, Y'all. It just makes me want to do a true happy dance. I love knowing that my navigational guide (Jesus) has already seen the beginning from the end, and he knows exactly where I am going, and when I will arrive at my destination.

He keeps us in perfect peace. How awesome is that? Perfect peace. He will overflow you in his peace not as the world gives but as only Jesus gives (John 14:27 and 16:33). Marvelous! Thank you, Jesus. Glory to God! Hallelujah! Thank you, Jesus, for your perfect peace that surpasses all understanding, that I can rest in your peace knowing you have covered me on all sides.

That no weapons formed against me shall prosper (Isaiah 54:17). Thank you, Jesus, I can rest in your peace knowing that I am not big or bad enough to stop what you have in store for me, that no one can have what you put my name on. What you have set aside for me is just for me. Thank you, Lord, that I can only delay my blessing because I have taken my focus off you and put it on something else for a moment, but I can in no way prevent or hinder your blessings for my life in any way. Thank you, Jesus!

The blessings of the Lord cannot be stopped by anyone. A delay is only a delay, and we bring that upon ourselves. The promises he's spoken over and in you will come to pass, and I know that because his word tells me so! When we get in our own way, he will hold it up, so we learn the lessons that need learning. Then we get back on course and chug along.

For me it started out with, "I think I can do this but I don't know if I will succeed." I was full of doubt. Not just doubting God, but doubting what he had placed in me. I question him still to this day. I'm like, "Are you sure God that you made the right choice? You really did mean to pick me, right?" He usually laughs and always reaffirms me. He knows my struggles internally.

It moved on from there to "Sure, I can do this look at me go." This time it was fear. I was scared to let all he placed in me out. The story in the Bible that Jesus told about the master giving three servants the talents of money in Matthew 25, I did not want to be like the guy who hid the talent of money in the dirt. I forge on with the Lord by my side, trusting in him that he has already equipped me to handle anything that may arise.

Now my current thoughts are "I'm doing this, and I am not letting anything stand in my way any longer. This has got to come out of my spirit to the flesh. People need to hear God's word. Now is the time." I was made to do what I am doing. I never saw that coming. That was truly a blindside. A great blindside, but scary nonetheless. I did not see me as a person God would use, let alone bless, in a massive way. I never thought I could be someone he would call up and send to the ends of the earth to do his work. Come on, I am just Sara. No one special in the world's eyes. Just little ole me. Did you catch that "world" comment? Therein lies the problem. Jesus doesn't bless, gift, or place talents in us as the world does. No, he does what only he can do. We are not of the world, we are only in the world. We are Kingdom kids. We belong to the ultimate King. The King of Kings. The Lord of Lords. Don't let anyone tell you otherwise. You got me! Repeat after me, *I am a KING'S KID*! (No matter your age.)

Romans 8:14–17 NLT: For all who are led by the Spirit of God are children of God. So you should not be like cowering, fearful slaves. You should behave instead like God's very own children, adopted into his family—calling him "Father, dear Father." For his Holy Spirit speaks to us deep in our hearts and tells us that we are God's children. And sense we are his children we will share his treasures—for everything God gives to his Son, Christ, is ours, too. If we are to share his glory, we must also share his suffering.

(I put this scripture right here just for you, so you can read the word of God and see just one of the many things he calls you. He truly, without any doubt, calls you his child. You are his beloved.)

The blessing journey in a nutshell. A lot goes into it, more than you even realize at the time. On the other side of the journey, I look back and think in true amazement, excitement, gratitude, and thanksgiving for how far God has brought me. Looking at all the growth, changes, being broken and then mended, being set free, and everything that life has thrown at me, I see how far I've come with Jesus, and it just blows my mind.

I think of all that was in me that Jesus took away and replaced with himself. It happens right in front of your very own eyes, and then one day, you realize the glorious change. You become awestruck by Jesus. It's wonderful!

Pray this with me. Thank you, Father. Thank you for creating and molding me into your child and your well-planned creation. Help me, Lord, give you control every day when I wake up and keep it in your hands throughout my whole day. With you at the helm, Lord, I can't go wrong. With you, Lord, I am blessed, favored, loved, cherished, and completely worthy to be yours. Amen.

It's that simple. Praying doesn't require skill, only true openness. Openness to allow Jesus into your heart. Don't be afraid to let him into every area of your life. He knows everything anyway, so why not let him have total access to you? Let him work in and through you every day. He's got this completely covered.

Hebrews 4:13 NLT: Nothing in all creation is hidden from God. Everything is naked and exposed before his eyes, and he is the one to whom we are accountable.

Reflection Questions

1. Did you stop fighting? What caused you to lose heart? You gave God your yes, so are you going to get back up and fight?
2. What are the desires of your heart? Have you asked the Lord for guidance how to fulfill them? Have you asked him what steps to take next to see them come to pass?
3. Are you remaining the clay in the Potter's hands or are you trying to be the Potter?

4. What part of the spectrum are you on when it comes to doing the will of God in your life? I think I can. Sure I can. I'm doing this.
5. Do you look back and see what God's done in you and through you? Do you see the previous blessings that encourage you to keep moving forward?

CHAPTER SEVEN

Extending Mercy, Because That's What You Do.

Isaiah 40:31 NLT: But those who wait on the Lord will find new strength. They will fly high on wings like eagles. They will run and not grow weary. They will walk and not faint.

Romans 12:8 NLT: If your gift is to encourage others do it! If you have money, share it generously. If God has given you leadership ability, take the responsibility seriously. And if you have a gift for showing kindness to others, do it gladly.

That's a fact, Jack. You extend mercy and grace to everyone you encounter. It's showing the kindness of the Lord to everyone. You are the light of God every day and everywhere you go. It's part of your job description and your assignment. If you're an encouraging person, be that to everyone you meet. If you are a person that shows kindness, do that, but do it to everyone you encounter. Don't keep those things locked up for only the ones you know and love.

Make an impact in this world with the gifts God's placed in you and do them gladly. God loves us to be cheerful. He says that many times in the Bible. He wants us to be of good courage (Joshua 1:9).

We must trust God to unlock every gift in us at just the right time. When we allow him to unlock the gifts in us, we begin to walk more fully in God's will for our lives. You are going to be making a Kingdom impact. Our gifts are locked up inside of us, and we don't have the keys to unlock them until the Lord teaches us the keys he's given us. You know you can't unlock a door without the correct key, so you must seek God for the keys. That's not always easy because we make excuses to keep us from reading our Bible, or going to church, or listening or watching Christian television or radio. We do it out of laziness, and we just don't want Jesus all up in our business because we are hurt, embarrassed, or we think he wronged us in some way.

Let's be honest with ourselves. At what point in your life is Jesus, your relationship with him, your present, and your future going to become the most important thing in your life? Jesus is the one that holds you in his hands.

Courage is doing something even though you are afraid. Courage is not absence of fear, but to do it in spite of your fear. Never let fear dictate your life. Mercy is having compassion or forgiveness toward someone whom it is within one's power to punish or harm. Grace is unmerited favor. Mercy is God not punishing us as our sins deserve, and Grace is God blessing us despite the fact that we do not deserve it. Mercy is deliverance from judgement. Grace is extending kindness to the unworthy. We can never earn either of these from God. They are a free gift to us daily, just like salvation. Gifts are things given willingly to someone without payment and/or an ability or talent. Blessings are when he gives us a generous amount of both grace and mercy. It's great knowing that the things the Lord gives and placed in us before we were ever thought of are so wonderful!

I know I keep saying this, but for me, it was at the age of thirty-one. I will continue to say, I never saw that coming. I am serious about that because I never figured I would have a relationship with the Lord. I thought that was an "old person" thing. I didn't realize in my little bubble how important that goal should have been until Jesus came busting through the door. I didn't realize that my prayer life had changed two years prior to that transitional moment. I was so tired of wondering what else this life held for me, and was this all there was to life (the constant struggle with worry, fear, and feeling worthless and like complete nothingness and useless)? Jesus is the most important person in my life. I talk about him like a mom talks about her kids, or a wife talks about her husband. I love Jesus. He is my everything, and my life will never work without him because this world is just too big for me to be on my own.

When we seek Jesus and he starts handing us keys to these hidden doors on the inside of us, he shows us how to use them. We then unlock even more of our potential, but it only comes from God. You are not in control of this process, Jesus is. No one's process is the same either.

You can't be in a hurry to figure everything out. Have patience in the Lord and his timing, but you also have to have patience with yourself. He won't hurry just because we are in a hurry. He takes baby steps to get us to certain places, in certain seasons, and in other seasons we grow leaps and bounds. It all depends on the season and our willingness to say yes to do all the work in us and with us, via the Holy Spirit.

It is your walk with the Lord. Take your time and enjoy the journey. Your walk is different than anyone you know. Jesus created us all differently on purpose. You are not a one-in-a-million. You are a one-of-one. There is no one else more you than you. You are an individual, and people may copy you, but they can never be you.

Write this down, or if you have a great and vast memory, remember this: I am a daughter/son of God. A joint heir with Jesus. A seed of Abraham. This is your identity in Christ. People will try to get you to question your identity, but remember in those times, when it is being questioned, you are a child of the most high God. This happens when you walk with Jesus. It's not a one-time thing you must tell yourself, because when you are walking with Jesus, this comes up. Jesus will never question your identity. He knows who he created you to be. The evil one is always trying to get you to falter (Romans 8:14, 8:17, 9:6–9 NKJV).

This is very important to remember. You are a one-of-one. There will never be another you no matter what someone might say. They have a misconception of who they are and what they were created to do.

Ephesians 1:13–14 NLT: "And now you also have heard the truth, the Good News that God saves you. And when you believed in Christ, he identified you as his own by giving you the Holy Spirit, whom he promised long ago. The Spirit of God's guarantee that he will give us everything he promised and that he has purchased us to be his own people. This is just one more reason for us to praise our glorious God."

Operating in your gifts can be hard at first, but you grow and learn with each passing day how to use them. Using your gifts for others is the key. Your gifts are not for you, but for everyone else. They come from the Lord. He placed those gifts in you for your calling, purpose, destiny, reaching the lost, and growing the Kingdom of God.

I will give you an example of one of my gifts the Lord has pulled out of me. Writing this book. Boom (imaginary mic drop because I always wanted to drop a mic). That's not at any of you, that's at the evil one that tries to tell me I am nothing at least once a day. My grammar is mediocre at best, and my spelling, well, let's just take a moment and thank Jesus for giving the computer programmers the idea for spell check. My vocabulary is small, in my humble opinion. In spite of my own personal preserved shortcomings, the Lord has taken it to a level that blows my mind regularly. He has me use words that I don't even know what they mean until I look them up, and then I'm all like "Where did I learn that word?" I didn't even know what that meant, but wow, I used it right. *Woot.* I high-five myself. Doesn't everybody? Wait, nope, probably just a Sara thing to do.

In all honesty, the Lord had me start writing September 7, 2014. At first it freaked me out. I was shaking and crying because I did not know what was going on. It was new and different. The Lord was right there with me, but it was still very overwhelming. I believe after I wrote that page-long love note, I took a nap. I was that tired. I was tired in a way I had never felt before. I was tired in my spirit, which is far different than just being tired after working all day. I think that's why it says, "Renew your mind" in the Bible, and why we make that scripture so important to everyone we talk to about Jesus and the Bible. To soothe that tired feeling in my spirit, I have to add more word. I liken it to needing food in your physical body—you need spiritual food to feed your spiritual body. The more you use your gifts, the more you have to take time to recharge yourself so that you can operate at the level the Lord requires of you. He needs you to be on your A game. You are operating heavy machinery, and you have to be alert and about yourself to function properly.

Here is the first letter the Lord gave me. I knew I had to write this down. I didn't know why, and I sure didn't understand the purpose at the time of writing things down, but I do now. I write what the Lord speaks in my heart so that I can go back and read it again for encouragement. This wasn't an audible voice, it was all in my heart/spirit, and when this happens, I cannot stop writing until I feel the release in my spirit that I have written every word he wants written. I try to pause because my hand cramps, and what do you know? The cramp immediately goes away so I can continue in the moment with the Holy Spirit. I didn't know the majority of the scripture he had me write at the time. It's quite interesting to see how the word of God flows through us regularly. "Labor pains hurt. It's always darkest before the dawn, but when that baby comes, it's a celebration. Praise be to God, for he is my provider, my caregiver. Blessings from Heaven will rain down on you. Have patience, have faith, for I am with you, the Lord your God. I always provide a way for my little ones. Have faith in me, my child, for I am with you. You are not alone. The promises I give to you are from my Father. He will fulfill His promises for you and with you. Have faith in me, my child, for I am with you. Guard your heart from the evil one

and things. I love you, my child. I am not finished with you yet. I've given you my promise
(WORD). I always fulfill my promises. I am not
a liar. I am the Great I AM, the one true God,
the Lord your Savior. This trial is difficult, but
I promised to never leave you or forsake you.
I am the ultimate provider. I'm the Great I AM.
The one true King of Kings, Lord of Lords,
Jehovah-jireh. Have faith in me, my child. I
love you, says the Lord. I bless my children
with great gifts that only I can gift. Have faith
in me, for I am with you. Be not afraid. Fear
not, for I am the Lord speaking to you, the
apple of my eye. The children I chose for this
battle were you. I didn't lead you into the wil-
derness to rot. I had to equip you for what was
to come. You have pleased me, my child. You
have handled much in the least and that tells
me you will handle much in the great. Leaning
on me at every turn, no matter what happens,
no matter the trials. My gain is what you will
seek. Doing as I say!" See how many times the
Holy Spirit told me not to fear? I was scared
because I didn't know what was happening. I
was obedient to that still small voice and it was
very valuable in the long run.

Zechariah 2:8 KJV: For thus saith the Lord of hosts; After the
glory hath he sent me unto the nations which spoiled you: for he that
toucheth you toucheth the apple of his eye.

John 16:7 NLT: But in fact, it is best for you that I go away,
because if I don't the Advocate won't come. If I do go away, I will
send him to you. (The advocate is referring to the Holy Spirit in this
scripture).

John 16:12–15 NLT: There is so much more I want to tell you,
but you can't bear it now. When the Spirit of truth comes, he will

guide you into all truth. He will not speak on his own but will tell you what he has heard. He will tell you about the future. (The Spirit of truth is the Holy Spirit in this scripture).

The next time he had me write it was overwhelming. I'm pretty sure I took a nap after that one too, but it was easier. Easier in the sense that I kind of knew what was going to happen this time. It's been three years and what do you know? He pulls a book out of me. When he started pulling this word out of me, I was really scared and very insecure because of my own perceived shortcomings. My family actually informed me that this was not a sermon, but a book. I thought it was a sermon series. The word *book* shocked me in a scared kind of way. I thought, "I am not good enough to write a book. Lord, are you sure this is a book?" Within a week, I had five chapters done, all in the Lord's time, and me shocked to my core. Won't he do it?

I would have never experienced the greatness the Lord has thrusted upon me and pulled out of me if I hadn't been willing to give into him three years ago (when he had me start writing). Actually my whole life. I love that Jesus picked me to gift this ability to, but I don't take it lightly. It still scares me from time to time. I know why, because every now and then the evil one tries to imitate Jesus and tries to get me to write his word. Here is where growth, experience, knowledge, and wisdom come into play. Out of the two times the evil one has tried to access my gift, I knew it was him. He does not operate like my daddy, Jesus. When he tried to hijack my talent, I knew it was not the Lord. When the Lord gives me the words to speak or write, I am not hindered by outside forces. I am not even delayed. It just flows, and usually faster than I can type or write. With the evil one trying to get me to speak or write, I am hindered, and it doesn't even make sense. Usually, it is in the past tense. Jesus is always about the present and the future, and he never throws my past in my face. He will never throw your past in your face. He will never shame you for your past. There is a huge difference between correction and condemnation. Praise the Lord!

Correction is defined as the action or process of correcting something, or a change that rec-

tifies an error or inaccuracy. Condemnation is defined as the expression of very strong disapproval, or the action of condemning someone to a punishment, sentencing. In the Bible, it is pretty much the same definitions for both words. However, correction comes from God. I always say, it's like your parents teaching you as you were coming up and learning the rules of the house. We have to learn the ways of the Lord and his Kingdom. That's why we need correction. Condemnation is from the enemy. It's usually linked with guilt and shame. It likes to pop up in my life when I've done something that isn't always on the up and up. Like talking bad or gossiping about someone. Which is wrong. It's stuff like that, that you know is wrong, but you do it without thinking of the consequences. It can lead to feelings of worthlessness and an assortment of other feelings that bring you down. I've never felt worthless when the Lord has corrected me, but when the enemy slings shade at me, I do. Like I said in the earlier chapters of this book, to know the character of the person you are speaking about when it comes to knowing the difference between the two voices. Scriptures to read on condemnation are listed here: Matthew 23:1–36 and John 3:16–21. Scriptures to read on correction: 2 Timothy 3:16 NLT and Proverbs 3:11–12 NLT.

"*The purpose of the voice of condemnation is to push you away from his presence-that which is the very source of your victory. The purpose of the voice of conviction is to press you into the face of Christ*" (Bob Sorge in Priscilla Shirer's *Discerning the Voice of God*).

Romans 8:1 NKJV: There is therefore now no condemnation to those who are in Christ Jesus, who do not walk according to the flesh, but according to the Spirit.

Your hardest trials open your biggest gifts and talents. Trust that the trial is teaching you to open that door. That door leads to a prime opportunity far greater than you can imagine. It's not an easy walk, but it is a worthy road to travel. Trust in what gifts God has given you. You will know they are from him based on what they are. You know exactly what they are. There is no denying them either because they just flow out of you, like singing, dancing, helping people, leading people in praise and worship, or ministering to the little ones, and so on.

I remember the first time the Lord gave me a writing for a friend of mine, and of course the cherry on top, it occurred right in front of her. *Ding, ding, ding,* something new to experience. YAY! (She said with a sarcastic tone). I wrote faster than her mom, who is a dear friend of mine, could pull up the scripture. That was quite interesting and shocking for me because it was something new for the Lord to do. He likes to make us uncomfortable, and I think that is a big part of our everyday testing. It happened, and I cried. This was about a year and half after God unlocked and taught me this amazing gift. What an adventure. We all cried and hugged it out. It was amazing to see how my gift affected us all that day. He taught me my gift in private, how it worked, and how to operate in it before he ever allowed another human to see him in action through me. The same will occur with you and your gifts, and eventually, he will bring your gift to the public.

Jesus took me by surprise that day. What else took me by surprise was going to church the next Sunday and hearing my pastor speak on gifts, and how he has continued to teach on gifts. My pastor taught me that your gifts aren't for you, but for everyone you encounter. I'm thankful for that knowledge. It's amazing what the Lord has taught me with this ability. He blows my mind pretty much daily.

What I am trying to say is, don't be surprised when your gifts are opened up in you if people start taking notice of you, people close to you call on you for prayer, advice, or knowledge, and most importantly, that people will be drawn to you. There is a purpose for everything under the sun and that includes your gifts (Ecclesiastes 3:1–22). Don't take your gifts lightly. Trust the Lord to pull them out of you at just the right time, and be prepared to be educated by the Lord on how to use them and use them correctly. The Lord will never let you loose with these gifts until he is sure you know how to use them. Look at me. He gave me three years of training before he gave me this book, and before that, I had the test in front of one of my dearest friends and her daughter. Trust in the Lord and his timing, and I promise you he will unlock some wonderful, amazing, and mind-blowing gifts on the inside of you to further his Kingdom and help others in need.

Romans 8:25 NLT: But if we hope for what is still unseen by us, we wait for it with patience and composure.

Extend yourself mercy as you learn your gifts. You aren't going to get it the first five times. It's going to take a minute. Just give yourself time to learn all that you are gifted with as you discover them.

Reflection Questions

1. Are you showing the kindness of Jesus to others? Are you letting your light shine brightly like the city on a hill?
2. Is your relationship with Jesus in good standing? Have you pushed him away because of fear, worry, or doubt?
3. In regard to your gifts, what just flows out of you naturally? What comes completely natural to you?
4. Do you take your natural God-given abilities for granted? Why? (They are a blessing not a curse.)

CHAPTER EIGHT

The Wait Is Over

Proverbs 3:5–6 NLT: Trust in the Lord with all your heart; do not depend on your own understanding. Seek his will in all you do, and he will show you which path to take.

Psalms 31:14 NLT: But I trusted in, relied on, and was confident in you, O Lord; I said, You are my God.

Isaiah 60:22 NLT: When the time is right, I, the Lord, will make it happen.

Things you never thought you could do, or thought you were capable of doing, or flat out not good enough to do, you can do them all. You are more than capable to do anything you set your mind to, you just have to be fearless and bold to step out on a leap of faith.

Mark 9:23–24 NLT: What do you mean, If I can? Jesus asked. Anything is possible if a person believes. The father instantly replied, I Do believe, but help me not to doubt.

When God shows you the gifts he's placed on the inside of you, run toward them without hesitation or fear. Trust that God has opened that up to you. Don't fear the unknown because we have a known God.

The fact of the matter is that we have to trust in the Lord and what he's given us. Trust in his timing and in him to deliver us out of these circumstances. Trust that he has us in the palms of his hands. That no weapons formed against you shall prosper. That with God all things are possible. No man can stop you when you are on the path with Jesus. Doors may shut, but eventually one will be opened unto you. Keep the course with Jesus. It gets hard, and seems impossible, but we know differently. We know that God is for us, so who could ever be against us.

I have had weapons formed against me many times. People have lied about me more times than I can count. Situations I thought would turn around didn't turn around. I have had things happen that I have no clue as to why. In spite of all that has happened and gone down in my life, God still showed up on my behalf. God is still making a way where I see no way. There is a light at the end of the tunnel, and the light has a name, Jesus.

Things got really dark in my life, and everything looked like it was going to end in a horrible way and there was no way out, but I walked through. I may not have had a smile on my face, but I kept stepping because the only way out is through. The storm raged on, but I kept going. I had an ace up my sleeve. I had a praise, and I had the word of God on my side.

My praise was a whisper with tears flowing because I had just hit the fight of my life. Knocked down and dragged out. I didn't know what to do. I was seriously on autopilot. That should never stop your praise, but it does from time to time; however, it will come back to you when you least expect it to. It's hard to keep your voice when you are walking in a horrible, scary, dry, and dark valley. Your voice is your ultimate weapon. In Ephesians 6:10–18, Paul tells us to put on our whole armor, and that includes your two-edged sword. Your sword is you speaking the word of God. The Bible says the word is sharper than a two-edged sword. You must speak in that valley the word of God, and at some point, you are going to see God show up in a way you didn't see coming. You will begin to see God's hand in everything. It feels very small at first, then look out, it becomes blatantly obvious when Jesus is working in your situation and things start changing rapidly. Things become different for "no apparent reason."

Hebrews 4:12 NLT: For the word of God is alive and powerful. It is sharper than the sharpest two-edged sword, cutting between soul and spirit, between joint and marrow. It exposes our innermost thoughts and desires.

Time will be like a time warp. Time will feel as though it stands still, and in another second, it will feel like you hit warp speed straight ahead. Be patient and of good courage because this too shall pass. This battle will run out of fuel. This storm will run out of rain. The valley will become plush with grass and flowers, overflowing in light with lessons learned and knowledge gained, and you, my friend, will be thriving like you never have before.

You have achieved a new level. A new level of maturity, knowledge, wisdom, understanding, loving-kindness, peace, joy, and increase. You have gone from the valley to the mountain top. God will show you where you've come from and where you are going. The wait is over. You now know that all you had to endure got you to the place the Lord needs and desires for you. A place that is far greater than you can fathom while you are in the valley of doom. It's not actually doom, but it sure does feel like it while you are there. Seeing that valley for what it was, and seeing the mountain top for the majesty and victory it has become, is a wild awakening in the depth of your spirit.

Please don't lose sight or hope or make your home in that valley. That is never where you were to stay. Yes, you feel like you are doing nothing right and you are stepping wrong and falling short every minute of the day, but you aren't, my child. You are growing, but you just can't see it yet. Have the peace that surpasses all understanding and be of good cheer. I know, I've been there, and it's not easy at the time. I know.

So many times I sat and just wept and cried, "Why? What is this all for? Why did you leave me? Why have you left me in complete darkness? Why do I have to do all this? This hurts, and I hate it! I hate being here! I miss my family and my friends! I have no one here. No one knows what I'm going through. I'm so lost. I have no clue what to do next."

My list felt endless when it came to my complaints, but it had an end. My praise, on the other hand, was endless because I have so much to be thankful for. Like my health. My family and friends—thank you, Jesus, I still have them, and I'll see them soon. The roof over my head and food on the table. Thank you, Jesus, for giving me the ability to prepare a meal that is wonderful and inexpensive. My dogs that I love to play with. The promises the Lord gave me before this valley. Thank you, Jesus, for toilets and running water. Thank you, Lord, for toilet paper. When you really think about it, the list of things to be grateful for is far longer than our lists of complaints (our complaints are the uncomfortable things we want corrected or changed immediately, problems with a solution we needed, like, yesterday).

I want you to know everyone has doubts, fears, and worries. No one is immune from those things. In the grand scheme of things, they are far outweighed every day by the grace of God. God has been with me every step of the way. He has his righteous right hand holding me up and some days holding me together when I feel like I'm going to lose it altogether. I'm far from perfect, but I am God's masterpiece. I remind myself regularly that I was fearfully and wonderfully made and that I am the apple of God's eye (Psalms 139:14), that Jesus loves me far beyond what I can comprehend this side of Heaven. That no matter what it looks like or whatever it may be that I am facing, God is with me and for me every step of the way. I can take that to the bank of knowledge and hold it there without any doubt, worry, or fear.

Ephesians 2:10 NLT: "For we are God's masterpiece. He has created us anew in Christ Jesus, so that we can do the good things he planned for us long ago."

I know that you are all on a journey with God, and I know they are all different, but we are all human and face the same challenges when it comes to worry, doubt, and fear. We are all imperfect humans, and we all have our races to run, but we can encourage each other along the way.

God will use you in ways you never saw coming, whether you're in the grocery store, gas station, or even on social media, to encourage others and make an impact in their lives. Trust that he knows what he is doing.

He will allow things to occur in your life to incite a season of uncomfortableness to grow you into someone better than you thought you could become. He knows our beginning from the end, and he knows what to do with us, through us, and in us, to get us where we need to be, doing what he created us to do. Entering into the uncomfortable seasons of your life are to grow you. Wait and hold on because it will be the wildest ride of your life and one of the best rides you'll ever have.

> **This is how I felt entering into my most uncomfortable season of my life to date. It wasn't easy, but it is not something I take for granted either. This really did happen in my life, but I only saw this in the spirit. It was a crazy time for me, but Jesus showed up in true Jesus fashion that dark night I sat alone in my room. This is what I felt in my spirit. Uncomfortable? Uncomfortable is an understatement. More like you've been beaten to a pulp, bruised, and bloodied sitting in a dark hole. Then Jesus walks in and you look up at him and cry out, "Fix it, Daddy," with your hands outstretched and your hands grabbing for him. He picks you up and carries you out like only a father can, and he whispers, "I am, and it's going to be far greater than you can fathom," as you feel a soft kiss brush your forehead. At that moment, the peace that only the Lord can give was poured in at an overflowing measure. That's what I've experienced in my last couple of years. When I cried out to the Lord in that state of uncomfortableness, I told him, "I cannot do this. This is hard, and it hurts too much." He wasn't joking when he had Paul write in Romans 8 that he works all things together for the good of those who love God. He is, and I see it now. He showed me many things that night about my future. I looked at the Lord and said, "You know me,**

right? Like, we've meet Lord. I'm spazzy, goofy, and even inappropriate, and you want me to do all that for you?" He laughed and smiled at me, and said, "You forget that I know you better than you know yourself, my child." Truth. I told the Lord, "You have to teach and show me how to walk this out because I've never been here before." He replied "I will. I will never leave you or forsake you, my child." Another bomb of truth. I say all that to say this growth is hard, and in certain seasons, it's ugly.

I don't know what your valley looks like, but I do know the mountaintop is majestic. Just hold on. The climb is worth it all. The view from there is amazing. When God shows you what he brought you through in its entirety, you will be amazed at just how awesome our God is and you are. You overcame that adversity. The darkness that you thought was going to overtake you failed, just as Jesus said it would. Look at you thriving and succeeding! You may not feel it in the valley, but you are successful, and you are more than a survivor of the ups and downs. You are a conqueror! You are a warrior! I know some days you feel as big as a mouse, spiritually speaking, but guess what? That is all lining up with Jesus, the author and finisher of your faith and life. With him residing in you and walking with you, you can't be defeated! It feels like it from time to time, but you are not a failure or defeated. The inside scoop is this: Jesus is not defeated or a failure in any way, and because he resides in you, neither are you.

You feel alone and secluded and that no one could possibly understand what you are going through, but that is just not true. You, my friend, are never alone. You are never ever alone. At times it feels like all hope is abandoned, but it's just slightly misplaced for the moment. A moment that can steal your joy, excitement, anticipation, happiness, and peace, but it can turn into something so magical. When I say magical, I mean that it can open your eyes to something far bigger than you can imagine, like the biggest praise you have ever released, and it's only a whisper, but it's all you have to give.

Like the woman in the Bible that gave her two pennies in the offering plate. That meant more to the Lord than the guy who gave a thousand pieces. It's all about the heart behind the giving. A pure heart will open doors you never imagined possible to open in your life (Luke 21:1–4).

That sacrificial praise meant more to God in that moment than you or I can comprehend. That was a big turning point in my life in that season of uncomfortableness. That praise opened my heart up to God in a new way, and Jesus made haste to fix, mend, heal, grow, change, and love me back to wholeness. He knows exactly what you are facing, and he is right there to do the same to you, through you, and with you. Don't hesitate to open your life and heart up to him. Be willing to be totally exposed to the Lord in that moment of uncomfortableness. Be willing to speak it to him. Watch him use it to make your life far better than you ever thought possible.

Without Jesus by your side, it is bleak, dry, and dark. With him, it's open, wide, and so bright—at least that's my own experience talking. Without the Lord by my side, everything I touched turned to junk, but eventually, I let him take all of me, and I haven't been let down yet. He never ceases to amaze me. He's always blowing my mind in some way or another.

Some days, I get down and feel defeated and worthless, but then someone comes along in true Jesus fashion and reminds me that is far from the truth. He will always send his ministering messengers to you at the perfect time to give you a boost out of the self-pity party. Let's be honest, that's exactly what it was, or is—a pity party. I have had my fair share of them, but Jesus never fails to show up and crash the party! He's done that through the people he's sent to me and sharing their love for me with me.

In your darkest moments, God will open up your greatest gifts. He uses that gift to show you the light at the end of the tunnel. To enlighten you of the vast amount of greatness he is thrusting upon you and pulling through you, for you to know and be encouraged to stay the course with Jesus. To keep on keeping on, even though it looks hopeless and dreadful to put one more step in the sand. To take another step would almost be soul-crushing and unbearable and so hard, but with each one of those hard, long, drawn out steps you'll begin to notice that one day it's not hard to take that step. Not anymore, anyway. Thank you, Jesus!

Getting to that point is long and feels like it's never ending, but it does have an end date. God won't leave you in this season forever. The seasons of uncomfortableness will fade, but only after you have learned every little thing you needed to learn, and you'll still be learning well after it's over.

The neat thing about life is that you look back with a different perspective, and you learn even more lessons. You grow even more. Your level of thanksgiving and gratitude grows more and more with each passing season. Like my momma always says, hindsight is always 20/20.

It's a wonderful thing to experience, but it really hurts, and you want to give up and give in, but then you think if you do that, then you're still stuck "here." Wherever "here" may be for you. My "here" was not the most fun place to be, but it did serve its purpose.

My advice is to hold on, keep stepping, pray, and seek Jesus, because he's the only one who holds time and the answers to all your questions. Don't give up! Don't give in to the pressures of the uncomfortable seasons. We have much to learn, and now is the time to learn.

I will leave you with some sound advice from my momma. "Ain't no step for a stepper, and this is the season where you see only one set of footprints in the sand because Jesus is carrying us through." My momma taught me these as I grew up. She knew I needed to know there would be seasons and days like this and that I would always need an encouraging word. She wanted to make sure it was a sound word, and it is in my heart every day. No matter what you face, there really isn't a step a stepper can't take! Word, truth, and knowledge you can take to the bank.

Reflection Questions

1. Have weapons formed against you? Did they appear to prosper? Did you look back and see where God stepped in and turned it for your good and his glory?

2. Are you thankful for the little things? Are you overflowing in gratitude and thanksgiving even though it looks so bleak? Why not? (There is so much to be grateful and thankful for even when you don't see it that way.)

3. Are you in a season of uncomfortableness? What have you been reading and learning in this season? Are you applying it in your everyday life?

4. Do you feel like you're isolated or secluded all by yourself in the uncomfortableness? Are you throwing a pity party? Have you asked the Lord, "What are you trying to teach me in all of this?" (Lean into it and learn, sugar. You're about to experience a massive growth spurt.)

5. Where is your "here?" Do you want out of the "here?" Are you taking the steps of faith God is speaking in the depths of your heart?

CHAPTER NINE

Let It Go: Breaking Up with Your Past

John 8:36 KJV: If the Son therefore shall make you free, ye shall be free indeed.

The past has nothing new to say. Let go of your past now. Your past can only define you if you allow it to. Shall we talk in depth about the past and the importance of letting it go? I think we should, so let's get to it.

I have told you some of my past, and it is not the prettiest of pasts, but it is mine. I have learned many things from my past, like my likes and dislikes and what I want for my life and what I will not allow in my life anymore. I learned from my past and allow it to be used in my life as an educational montage from time to time. It's a "what not to do or be when you grow up" kind of thing for me.

It's hard to write this chapter knowing that I am going into detail about my past. Some of those things I wish never happened, and some of them I don't even remember happening to me. Here it goes, and please don't judge me because I am human and wasn't always the smartest of humans either.

I want to see people set free from their past, just as I want to be free of my past. Yes, it happened, and there is no denying that and no point in hiding it either. It happened. Just let that sink in...my past happened.

I want you to know your past does not in any way, shape, or form define you. It's a long line of choices we've made that have in some ways shaped us into who we are. Some of those things are not actually who we were meant to be. Those things of the past cannot go where we're going, so it's best to deal with them now before we get to that next level or destination, if you will. Those things have to be broken off now so you can grow and bloom into who you were fully created and meant to be. Don't let it hold you back any longer.

Now is the time to be set free, allowing Jesus to break every chain holding you back, because in Jesus, we are free. Free to be molded into who he actually created us to be. He is the Potter, and we are the clay. Let's be the clay and let him be the Potter. In the Potter's hands is where I want to be. Let's get free from the past. Let's live in the freedom of Christ Jesus (Isaiah 29:16).

I had a dream the other day. It was weird, but now looking back at that dream with Jesus, I had an eye-opening experience. In the dream, I had a four-story house. I had the master bedroom in the basement. The curtains were sky blue so they blended in with the walls. The walls were a slightly lighter blue with clouds painted towards the ceiling. White, fluffy, soft carpet, soft like a kitty, soft. The room was very organized and spotless clean. No dirt or garbage anywhere. Everything was neat and tidy, like I like it to be.

I walked to the next level, and it was the kitchen, living room, and dining room area. The kitchen was the only part that was a mess. There was contact paper on all the counters and tabletops. The contact paper was ripped and torn, with parts missing. As I inspected this, I found layers of grease in between the layers of contact paper. Liquid grease with chunks of food and flour mixed together. It was disgusting. I pulled all the contact paper up and cleaned feverishly. I was able to get the actual surface of all the counters and tabletops degreased and clean.

I have no clue what was on the third level of the house except that it was my parents' floor.

I walked to the top floor. It was a couple of bedrooms. One was a guy's room full of dirty clothes and empty juice bottles. I did all the laundry and threw the bottles away.

The other bedroom was much weirder. I opened the door, and it was total darkness. I turned on the light to look around. There was a young man, like ten- to twelve-year-old boy, with a five-year-old girl that looked like me. I told them they had to leave. Then I could only see what was floor-to-ceiling full of boxes. It looked like old board games and stacks of boxes in various sizes and colors. Some were pink, orange, purple, and blue. In one corner was a very small twin bed, not made, just a mess of blankets and sheets and a ratty old brown and yellow pillow.

I knew in my spirit in the dream that I had to pray over this room. Something wasn't right about this room. I began praying and speaking the word of God over this weird room in my house. Out of nowhere came this crazy, strong, knock-you-down kind of wind from the closet. The wind was so strong, it knocked me off my feet and threw me backwards about four feet, and the room was full of darkness once again.

I get up and charge the doorway, and I am screaming over the room, "This room is clear in Jesus' name," over and over and over. Then my dad walks up behind me and says, "Charged." That's when I woke up.

I tell you my dream to tell you that the only significant part is the last room. It's part of my spiritual house that I needed to clean out. Don't lose focus and count me as a nut job just yet, mmmkay?

Looking back now, about five days later, I remember that when I charged the room and was screaming, the room was empty. What I realized is that little girl was me, and that boy in that room was the boy who molested me when I was a child. Thank you, Jesus, for my big brother because he witnessed the act and told my momma. She missed like a week of work, I think, to get us into a different daycare after that incident.

I don't remember a whole lot of my childhood, from about ten to twelve and younger. From what I am told, it was pretty bad. The only reason I knew it was that boy was because of the Holy Spirit informing me. It's a blessing really in my opinion, and I wish others had the same blessing of lack of memory when it comes to this stuff. If I remembered all the things my family tells me about my childhood, I think I would be very bitter, mean, hateful, and a downright awful human being, and I probably wouldn't have let Jesus into my life either.

The things I do remember for the most part are good, and fun, and funny. Things like riding my bike chasing after my big brother and playing G.I. Joes with him. Watching my momma get her hair done at the salon, which intrigued me so much that I went to hair school. One of my many favorites is dancing around my Memaw's apartment with her and my brother to the record player cranking out the old classics. The bad stuff I don't remember for the most part.

I have anger issues, and when things like this pop up in my memory bank, they incite hurt, and anger follows. I am not angry at my mom, my dad, or my brother because of this incident, but I'm angry because that little boy thought that was okay to do. Thankfully, it only happened to me the one time. How I wish others could be so "lucky." Once is one too many times, let alone the years some people experience. To those men and women that have experienced this, I am sorry someone thought they had the right to do that to you. It wasn't okay, and it is not your fault it happened to you. I pray that through the Holy Spirit one day you can forgive and let it go in the aspect that you are not what happened to you. Yes, it changed your course, but it cannot define you unless you let it. Forgiveness is for your health, and it in no way means that it is you saying it was okay, that whoever did this to you should not be punished for what they did to you. I pray the Lord will fill you with his peace and help you forgive them so you can move on and help others.

That bedroom in my dream was my past that I don't remember and that I had somehow locked it away. It being empty when I charged back to the door screaming like a nut job was showing me that Jesus had already, that quickly, taken it away. That in a matter of seconds, Jesus takes the past away and covers it with his blood and love. That my past, of what I can only imagine was awful, and painful, and terrible, was now gone and covered. That was from my actual youth that I didn't even know was hidden inside of me.

In 2014, my dad ordered a series from Pastor Robert Morris called *Free Indeed*. Little did my dad know that one purchase would change my life. In that series, Pastor Morris talked about getting free from anything and everything in your life that was, or is, holding you back or down.

The last message is where God met me and began my freedom process. The last message is "Open Gates, Set Free." (Sermon series called *Free Indeed*.) In that final message, Pastor prayed that the Holy Spirit would show you where you needed to be set free. I prayed with him, and the Holy Spirit did just that. The Holy Spirit showed me people I needed to forgive and release from me. People that I didn't even know that I needed to forgive. That was the day the Lord showed me that I was molested by a boy at my daycare.

My mom and my brother have talked with me a few times, seeing if I remember the event, and I don't. After I forgave that boy, the Lord took the memory away again. The Lord is the only reason I knew in that dream who that boy was.

I count my lack of memory of my childhood a blessing because it can't be thrown in my face. I don't have the option to keep reliving the event. I thank the Lord that it only happened the one time. Now the childhood and adult life choices I remember are the ones I wish I could forget but cannot. They are the things that get thrown in my face, which feels like daily. Like my drinking and smoking pot and the horrible decisions I made while intoxicated, like driving drunk. Reading books that gave me the heebie-jeebies and watching things that do the same, like movies or TV shows filled with all kinds of evil. The ones that get me the most are the awful words I spoke to and over people, and not standing up when I saw injustices being done. I didn't always love people or treat the ones I love right. I am far from perfect.

I can say I don't want to be perfect because that takes more energy than I am willing to give, in all honesty. However, we are made perfect in Jesus. He qualifies us to be perfect in him and not of our own doing either. He washes us clean. He takes our pasts and turns them around, qualifying us to do what we are called to do by him. (See Colossians 1–4 for more in depth reading on this subject. I promise you won't be disappointed.)

We have no control over the past. Once it's done, it's done. There is no undo button, even though we wish there was. What's in our best interest is to let it go and let Jesus set us free from our past, good, bad, ugly, or indifferent. What we have to do is lay it at the feet of Jesus and leave it there. Stop picking it up and trying to carry it again. We weren't meant to carry it, so just leave it at his feet (easier said than done, but it can be done). Every time you find yourself trying to pick it up, just say, "No, I trust you, Lord, and I know you've got this." I have to tell myself this regularly, and some days many times a day.

The Lord had Paul write in Romans 8:31–37 that nothing can separate us from the love of the Lord. Not even your past can keep you from the Lord. Hear me, the enemy will try to tell you otherwise. The evil one will try to tell you that you are unworthy, of no value, you are nothing, and that Jesus doesn't even love you because _____. He's tried, and tried, and tried to do that to me, whether a whisper in my ear or someone speaking to me.

For example, a friend of mine said, "You're pretty, but I am beautiful." In my opinion, we are all beautiful. I don't care who you are, you're beautiful. Or the whispers in my ear: *You aren't good enough for a man to love you because you aren't close enough to Jesus, and you aren't smart or educated enough, you don't give enough.* On and on and on, like a broken record. It gets downright annoying, and it angers me because I know differently.

Jesus says (this is the truth I stand on and it's in the Bible) I am a masterpiece, beautiful, and made in his image, smart, educated, worthy of love, and most importantly, *His* love. I do have a relationship with Jesus, and it's always growing and changing into something more every day. I give more than I realize. The still small voice in our hearts speak these truths and wonderful words over us daily. When you know your past is forgiven, but the enemy tries to throw it in your face, just remember what Jesus says about you. Speak those beautiful words over yourself out loud.

Meditate on the word of God, which is speaking the word over and over and over again to yourself, whether it be internal or external. Your past will try to keep you down and out. It will try to hold you back from the promises God has given you, but remember God is for you. You are forgiven. You are set free. You are free. You are redeemed, restored, renewed, and refueled by Jesus daily. The blood of Jesus covers a multitude of sin (1 Peter 4:8). Whom the son sets free is free indeed (John 8:36).

We conquer evil by doing good (Romans 12:21). Whatever your past may be, don't let it hold you back any longer. Let it go and live in freedom. It's covered. You're covered. It's done. It literally can't do anything to you any longer.

One thing my pastor taught me a while ago was this, and I am reminded of it often, "Jesus loved you when your past was still your future." It's the truth. The Lord loves us more than we can fathom this side of Heaven in spite of our past, present, and future.

I want you to trust God to cover and remove your past. He can do all things, but it's up to us to give him the "yes" and the opportunity to go to work on and in us. We have to be willing to open that bedroom door to allow the Lord in and let him do his thing. I honestly didn't realize it was that quick and easy to open up to him until I had that dream a few days ago. It just happened, and I didn't hesitate to let Jesus in my whole heart. I didn't realize that my house wasn't completely in order. Now I know it is, and it's sealed up by the Lord. I had to open up completely to the Lord and I had to be willing to let him work. The best way he found with me was in my sleep. I'll take the Lord any way I can have him.

That dream was so vivid it felt like I was awake. It was something that the Lord used to get my undivided attention, and it worked. I'm thankful he knows how to get our attention and hold it like he does. He never fails to show up when I need him, which is every day. He always knows what I need and when I need it most.

The freedom I've experienced these last few years and days has been liberating. Feeling my chains being broken off me, I feel lighter on the inside. I feel my spirit doing back flips, and dancing and singing. It's not uncommon for me to feel this way on a regular basis because it's becoming my new normal, and I love it!

With every chain link that has tried to hold me back I press on and push forward. I refuse to allow something I cannot undo hold me hostage any longer. I have too much I want to see and do to allow the fear of my past to keep me from my future. The Lord has told me tidbits of my future, and I am ready to get to it and see what all Jesus has in store for me and my life. I refuse to be a hostage in my own body any longer. I put my foot down and drew my line in the sand many years ago, and to give up after making it this far would be beyond regretful.

I want you all to experience the freedom to be unafraid of what your present and future holds. I want you to get up boldly every day and feel alive and live your life to the fullest giving God all the glory. I want you to live your life without doubt, worry, or fear and that's what Jesus says to us every day. Every day he says, "I love you, my dear beautiful little child, you are my lovely masterpiece, and you my friend are going to do amazing things with me today!"

We just need to stay focused on the Lord and watch him work through us and with us. Along the way, your chains will be broken, you will walk in freedom. You will find yourself living a life you never dreamed of because you didn't even know it was possible. How awesome is that!

The list of possibilities are endless. To see Jesus show up in our lives is amazing. Along the way he shows us some of the most amazing, wonderful, and beautiful moments of life. To see his hands at work in everything that involves us is mind blowing. To see him caring for others through us and watching him show others love through us just makes me happy, excited, and energized to keep going and doing more. To be the light, a city on a hill, to show others that God is in control makes me almost want to jump out of my body (Matthew 5:14 and Psalms 119:105).

I love to watch God work. He is truly an artist. I see the beauty in others just waiting to be unleashed, and it's awesome to watch him unlock that in them. He is truly my hero for all he does in my life. The way he extends mercy and grace to us every day is a song to my heart. A song that is on repeat every day! Thank you, Jesus!

Get up in your freedom and know you are free. Free from the things that try to hold you down and hinder you. You are free to be who the Lord actually created you to be. Walk in that truth and know it is happening. The Lord is working on us daily whether we know it right at this moment or not. He is working for us in every way possible. Jesus is interceding on our behalf. Our names are on his heart and lips daily. He knows exactly what you need and when you need it most. Rely on him to let you know what's going on, and trust that he will tell and show you.

Isaiah 49:16 NLT: See, I have written your name on the palms of my hands. Always in my mind is a picture of Jerusalem's walls in ruins.

Pray this with me: Dear Lord Jesus, help me hear you clearly and feel your presence in this journey. Help me know without a doubt it is you speaking to me. Give me a dream, a vision, a word from a trusted person, or help me stay still and quiet long enough to hear you speaking to me. Set me free from my past. Lord, I allow you through the Holy Spirit to come into my life and break every chain holding me down. Lord, I allow you to deliver me from every addiction that is holding me back. I ask that you would come and be a part of my everyday life, to be in the forefront of my mind helping me make the correct decisions. Remove my shackles and help me get set free from my bad decisions, the misfortune that has been bestowed upon me, the things people inflicted upon me to keep me down and away from you, Lord Jesus. Seal my past and remove it from me. Help me see the beauty from my ashes. Lord, help me see me the way you see me, FREE. Help me give you control to right my course. I ask that you would allow the Holy Spirit to go to work in me showing me what I need to do, set me free from everything hindering me, and help me stay willing to work through this with you. Be my guide as your word says you are. Show me where I need to extend forgiveness and release people from me and my past. Bring to my mind what I need to do to let my past go. Lord, comfort me as I allow you to work on and in me. Lord, hold me together, as I feel like I am falling apart at the seams. Help me become the clay in your hands and help me give you the Potter position in my life. I want to be free, and free indeed. Lord, help me feel you working on and in me. Help me focus on you through all of this. Help me get free and stay free. Lord, help me trust in you that my past is forgiven and covered by your precious blood. Father, help me have this freedom revelation in my heart, not just my head. Help me seek you in this freedom journey. Lord, I know now that I am free, and free indeed, just as your word says. Thank you, Jesus, for breaking my chains and setting me free. Thank you, Lord Jesus for being with me through all of this. Thank you, Jesus. All this I ask and pray in Jesus' name, Amen.

You can shrink this down to what you need for your life. You don't have to pray this whole prayer if only parts of it include you. Mold it into your life and your life experiences. The Holy Spirit will guide you through this prayer, or the one he gives you just for you. The same can be said with the following word to speak over yourselves.

Now speak this with me: I take authority over the lust of the flesh and eyes, sexual immorality, impure thoughts, lust, in Jesus' name. I take authority over the drug and alcohol addictions right now, in Jesus' name. I take authority over the addictions to food, anorexia, and bulimia right now in Jesus' name. Anorexia and bulimia, you no longer have a foot hold on, or over, these people. No longer will you use food as a weapon on them, in Jesus' name. I take authority over pornography right now, in Jesus' name. Pornography will no longer be your guide in sexual relations. It can no longer define you as a man or a woman. It has no hold over you any longer, in Jesus' name. I take authority over misuse of money and the lack thereof, right now, in Jesus' name. I take authority over abusive language right now, in Jesus' name. I take authority over the unclean spirits trying to harm you physically right now, in Jesus' name. No longer will you face suicide, in Jesus' name. No longer will the thoughts of suicide be able to keep you stuck in a closet contemplating death and that you don't matter, because you do matter, in Jesus' name, you matter. Right now, in Jesus' name, I bind: lust of the flesh and eyes, sexual immorality, impure thoughts, drug and alcohol addictions, addictions to food, anorexia and bulimia, pornography, money problems, abusive language, suicide and unclean spirits, I bind these things off you right now, in Jesus' name. I cast all of these things off you right now, in Jesus' name. You can no longer hold these children down any longer, Satan, in Jesus' name. You must flee from them, Satan, right now, in Jesus' mighty name. I plead the blood of Jesus over every person reading this book right now, that they may be free. They are blood bought and paid for by Jesus. Satan, you must leave them now, in Jesus' name. No longer will you try to convince them they are unworthy of the Lord Jesus Christ's love for them. No longer can you hold them down and away from Jesus Christ. It is written that **NOTHING** can separate us from God's love. No mistake or sin can keep us away from Jesus. It is written, we are free to boldly come to Christ. It is written that no weapon formed against us shall prosper, no harm shall befall us, in Jesus' name. In Jesus' name I pray, AMEN.

If you need to go more in depth on this prayer, or taking authority over things in your life past, present, or even in the future, just build on this foundation. Read in Matthew 12:22–37 and Matthew 16:13–20. This is actually Jesus explaining everything I have just written for you and me. In Matthew 18:19–20, "I also tell you this: If two of you agree down here on earth concerning anything you ask, my Father in Heaven will do it for you. For where two or three gather together because they are mine, I am there among them." This scripture helps me regularly, especially when I am asking for help and prayer. If we are praying together in one accord (praying the same way for something), then we are together with the Lord. You and the Holy Spirit in one accord is okay too. Some days you will need this because some days you just get ambushed by crazy thoughts. Don't worry because *You* got this, because *Jesus* has you!

You do not have to pray that really long prayer every time you need to pray over yourself. Edit it down to your needs. Allow the Holy Spirit to show you how to use this prayer pattern to your advantage in your everyday life. This prayer of mine was, and is, to help anyone and everyone that touches this book. To show them that I, too, am praying over and for them, not just for myself.

If you need help with any one of these things listed above, do not be afraid to seek out counsel. God will guide you to the appropriate people or person to help you fully overcome anything that is coming against you. He's already educated someone to help you. Take a leap of faith and seek out that help if you need it and do not be ashamed to ask for help. We all need council from time to time, and the Lord knows that is the case, but ultimately, he wants you to build your faith and trust in him. Seek the help you need, but seek Jesus at the same time.

These next few scriptures prove that God wants you to seek the council you need. Please, please, please do not fear asking for help. I know for me I have an issue asking for help from time to time because I have an issue with pride. Something that I am working on and really am moving past, but I always know when I am at the end of me and I have to break down and ask for help. I ask for help more than I ever have in life. I don't want you to hesitate asking for help. Please get the help you need!

Psalms 1:1 KJV: "Blessed is the man that walketh not in the counsel of the ungodly, nor standeth in the way of sinners, nor sitteth in the seat of the scornful."

Proverbs 11:14 KJV: "Where no counsel is, the people fall: but in the multitude of counsellors there is safety."

Philippians 3:13–15 KJV: "Brethren, I count not myself to have apprehended: but this one thing I do, forgetting those things which are behind and reaching forth unto those things which are before, I press toward the mark for the prize of the high calling of God in Christ Jesus. Let us therefore, as many as be perfect, be thus minded: and if in anything ye be otherwise minded, God shall reveal even this unto you."

You are loved and cherished and you are a treasure. You are his beloved. You are his child. Your past has nothing new to say any longer. You, my friend, are on your way to being set FREE!

> **I want you to hear me. This is important. This chapter may have caused you more pain, or even anger, at my audacity to say you can move past the past. Some say your past is a badge of honor to carry forward and be glad in it in some way. No, that isn't true. IT'S OKAY TO NOT BE OKAY. It's okay to seek help. I will tell you this, shame, guilt, and a number of other (unknown to me) reasons may try to keep you from seeking help,**

but push past those feelings. The simple fact is those things that have happened to you are not negated when you ask for help. They are not negated by pushing past your hurt. The fact of the matter is someone, somewhere, needs you. Needs you to get healed from that past. Baby, your story is going to help other people get set free because of how you stood up to the past and its violations against you. That what you experienced and got free of and overcame needs your life experience to minister to them. To show them that you can stand up and you can be the person God created you to be and not live in constant fear. You don't have to sit and have fear, worry, and doubt tell you that this is the day. This is the day you die. This is the day something awful is going to happen. No! No more. When you allow Jesus into your mess and he starts working on and in you, he teaches you along that road your power and authority in him (2 Timothy 1:7). When you decide to drop the title of victim and strap on the title of SURVIVOR, it's going to be one of the most beautiful days of your life. Yes, you were victimized, and it happened; however, you are more than the sum of that which happened to you. You are so much more than what happened to you. Baby, this world needs you! We need you and your strength, courage, bravery, and your wisdom. We need you! We need you to be you! We need you to stand up and tell your story to help another person just starting down this road you were on. To help them heal and be encouraged in the struggles. To be united and stand up for each other and in the gap for one another in prayer, making our petitions know to God.

"No matter what you are going through, someone else has faced it with Jesus and was victorious on the other side" (Pastor Ron Carpenter, Jr. Redemption Church).

I believe you are that victory story waiting for someone to see or hear, and God starts using it to heal and mend them.

Below are some lifelines you can use to start getting the help you need. I want you to be able to move past your past and these agencies below can help you with that process. They will not mock you or make fun of you. They are there to help you!

National Suicide Prevention Lifeline
1-800-273-8255, available twenty-four hours every day.
Crisis Support Services of Nevada (they can help with substance abuse, child abuse, and other situations)
1-800-273-8255 or Text CARE to 839863
Sexual Assault Help Line
1-775-221-7600
The National Domestic Violence Helpline
1-800-799-SAFE (7233)
National Teen Dating Abuse Helpline
1-866-331-9474
The National Human Trafficking Hotline (for the US)
1-888-373-7888
National Center for Missing and Exploited Children
1-800-843-5678
The National Eating Disorders Association (NEDA)
1-800-931-2237
Addiction Hotline
1-800-815-6308

Reflection Questions

1. What's God asking you to give him? What door is he knocking on in your heart?
2. Where is the Holy Spirit bringing your focus to in your past? What's in that room? What is it that is holding you

down and trying to suffocate you? Are there people he's calling out to you to forgive? What is he asking you to release into his care? What is holding you hostage?

3. What is the Holy Spirit telling you in your spirit to encourage you? Do you feel his comfort and peace overflowing in you? Are you meditating on God's word to gain his peace and presence? Is the Holy Spirit welcome in your atmosphere?

CHAPTER TEN

Gratitude. It's a Thing

According to Merriam-Webster's dictionary, *gratitude* is the "quality of being thankful; readiness to show appreciation for and to return kindness."

I love David. He's not afraid to say, "Jesus/Lord I have doubt and I feel like you've abandoned me, but I am still going to praise you, O Lord." He doesn't try to hide it. He has no problem letting the Lord work on him on the inside because let's face it, he was a fallible human just like us, but we can learn so much from David.

We can learn that in the midst of a storm, keep praying and praising, but I've already said that. What we need to do in the midst of a storm, or trials, or tribulations, is read our word/Bible. That's most important. We have to remember to speak God's word over our lives and the ones we love. It's so important to have that fresh renewing word wash over your insides. It's a healing balm to our hurting places, our broken places, our offended places, and our ouchies of the soul and spirit.

We need that living water of Jesus to be constantly rushing through us on a level we've maybe never experienced before. If we allow the living water that is Jesus wash over and through us on a daily basis, we'll begin to notice those sore spots are healing, or are already healed, and our broken places have scar tissue now, instead of being open, and hurting, and aching.

We have to allow Jesus to go to work on the inside of us daily. Allow him total access to our hidden places and allow him to bring them to the light, no longer satisfied in keeping those places hidden or out of reach.

It's time for healing. Healing from the top of your head to the tips of your toes. Your willingness and your "yes" to Jesus to get into those deep dark places of your soul and bring it to the surface to get it ultimately out of you. Total healing of your past hurts and mistakes.

Let's face it, we all have past hurts and mistakes we wish we could take back or give back to the one that caused it, but we cannot. We now have to deal with them through the Holy Spirit and allow him access to ultimately heal those open wounds. It gets messy, and you really hurt through this because on one hand, you don't want to deal with the pain again. On the other hand, it hurts and makes you sick to your stomach to even think about it coming back up to the surface. Staying hidden feels easier, but if we are honest with ourselves, deep down on the inside, we know we just don't want it anymore. None of it. Take it, you can have it back. That's how I feel with my stuff. That is how I felt through this process. It hurt, and I would try to shove it all back down and hide it all away.

Then one day I was just over that, let's call it what it is, the crap of my past. The bad and what felt like complete ugliness. I was tired of it rearing its ugly head. I was over that stuff crippling me. Whether it was fear or pain, it didn't matter any longer because I was done. I had hit my limit on hiding the mess.

Please hear me, it does hurt, and you do go through the gambit of emotions when the Holy Spirit is in there cleaning house, but it's worth it on the other side of this. It's called healing, forgiveness, grace, and mercy. Extend yourself grace and mercy as you go and grow through all of this. It's the only way I made it to the other side of becoming whole. You will get to a point, one day out of the blue, you will have that realization or revelation of wholeness. I realized one day I no longer felt broken. I no longer had that pit of anxiety in my stomach. I was no longer on edge. I realized the past and all its junk was done. Handled. Completed. Finished.

I want you to feel that exact same way. It's done. I am whole. I am healthy. I am healed! I am done with the past. I am moving on up! You can actually relax completely in your own skin. To rest without fear or worry. I want you to be able to sleep at night full of peace instead of worry. I want you to be unafraid to stand up and share your story one day because you took the time to get "cleaned up" on the inside. That now you are on the other side and you can help someone else that's struggling. Help them realize it doesn't have to be that way any longer. I want you to live in freedom to be who God created you to be. I want you to live unapologetically when it comes to your past because once you are free you no longer feel you have to apologize for it anymore.

Stop throwing your past in your own face. I have to tell myself that from time to time. The enemy of our spirits doesn't want us free or healed. He wants you broken and down, and he will go to any length to get you there and keep you there. <u>BUT</u> Jesus (notice there is always room for a "BUT God" moment) wants us free, healed, uplifted, living in our Jesus freely given righteousness. Jesus wants us whole, healed, and healthy. He doesn't want us to live backwards in our past. He wants us focused forward and our eyes fixed on him. He doesn't want us doubting our freedom or our healing. He wants us to walk in those completely.

You have to open the door to Jesus if you want that sweet release of freedom and healing. It took me a few years to go through this process because I kept closing myself off. I didn't want to bring all that back up. I didn't want to relive the mistakes. What I didn't realize is that when Jesus comes in and starts poking and picking at those places that really only he can truly see, the process is quick. He and I talked about them, and boom, they were covered.

For some people, however, the hurts run deeper. That's okay. Take your time in the quiet with Jesus and allow the Holy Spirit the proper amount of time in your hurts to ultimately heal those deep wounds. Some of those hurts didn't occur in just one day. Some took months or years to cultivate those wounds, so don't expect them to be healed immediately. In essence, it may take a while for you to feel the healing and shift in your heart. I am not going to judge you. I have said it time and time again, enjoy your journey with Jesus. Take your time and allow the Holy Spirit to do what only he can do. There really isn't a time limit on this process. It just takes the time it takes, but trust Jesus to do what is best in your heart and soul.

It's no one's business but yours while you're growing through all of this. When you are ready to share all of the Lord's work in you, he will show you what, where, and who to share with. I wanted to shout it from the roof tops. I wanted everyone to know what Jesus and the Holy Spirit had done in me. I wanted and want everyone to experience this healing and freedom for themselves. To wake up each day knowing that it's no longer over me. That I broke down those walls through the Holy Spirit and now I'm living healed and whole. I found contentment. Contentment I'd never known before. I heard about it but never lived it for myself.

In contentment I've found my biggest praise, joy, happiness, loving kindness, and peace. Now, no matter what I have, or where I live, I have contentment in my heart. Like Paul wrote, he knew what it was to have a full stomach or empty, having a lot or a little, it didn't matter, he was content in the Lord. Know that it's *not* settling. No, do not settle. What it is, is knowing whose you are, fully knowing you are loved, and cherished, and most importantly, you have Jesus. Nothing can change that.

Philippians 4:11–13 NLT: Not that I was ever in need, for I have learned how to be **content** with whatever I have. I know how to live on almost nothing or with everything. I have learned the secret of living in every situation, whether it is with a full stomach or empty, with plenty or little. For I can do everything through Christ who gives me strength.

A few months ago, I had an epiphany. I was standing outside my front door stargazing and realized in an instant that no matter what life may bring, I have all I need because I have Jesus. Even a year ago, I could not have said that and meant it truly because I was still healing. The road was dark, and I wanted to quit and give up because it was hard and it hurt, but what I realized a year ago is that I'd rather go through this now and be done. I wanted contentment. I wanted to know what that felt like and looked like in real life. I have it now, and I am so thankful. I realized for the last year, I think, I've called every major holiday Thanksgiving. I am overflowing in thanksgiving to the Lord for everything. I am talking coupons, running water, parking spaces, gas prices dropping, toilet paper, microwaves—you name it, I'm thankful.

I wasn't always like that. I took so many things and people for granted. I look back now and see that. I praise the Lord even more that those amazing people I took for granted are still there because they loved me through all of my mess. They knew Jesus would work on me and correct my mixed-up places. They prayed for me for all of it to be righted.

It's important to be mindful of who you allow access to you. You need your circle of people to be trustworthy, loving, and completely honest with you. You need that kind of support doing life. My trust circle is only five or so people. People I can count on to pray with and for me and love me through all of life.

In true contentment lies gratitude. Gratitude for everything under the sun because you appreciate everything Jesus does in your life and through your life. That he alters your life in amazing, new, and wonderful ways every day of your life. Without Jesus, you wouldn't know wholeness, or true happiness, or peace, or true love for that matter. Love that only Jesus can give you. That in Jesus you are complete with nothing missing, nothing lacking, and nothing needed. That's not to say you don't need things physically speaking, because you do. What I am talking about is spiritually speaking, you are missing nothing because in Jesus you have all that you need. Jesus gives you all you need to be able to do what he's called and created you to do.

I am talking all spiritually in this chapter. True contentment in Jesus. Jesus is everything to me. I got Jesus on my mind and my mind on Jesus. I want to be pleasing only to him, and if I am doing that, everything else falls into place perfectly in his time. It takes time. It doesn't happen overnight because we get in our own way. We limit the Lord from time to time. I think for most of us this is true.

We put stipulations on the Holy Spirit. You can have every room in this house, but you can't touch my junk drawer. What happens to us when someone tells us don't look down? What's the first thing we do? We look down. Same with the Holy Spirit. That's the most important part at one point in your life. You say, "No, Lord," and he says the inevitable, "Yes, Sara, you have to give it to me."

Let me tell you this from experience. The more you say "No," the more turmoil you will feel on the inside. The fight is real. We don't want that junk drawer fooled or fiddled with. It's locked down for a reason. The fear. The hurt. The scary things that happened could possibly creep back in and continue to hurt you. The loathing of oneself. The lack of confidence in the Lord to actually take the hurt, fear, poor self-worth, lacking in every way, and take the whole pain away. That right there is fear dictating your life. Have faith to take that one step he's asking you to take. That one small step of faith in God's eyes is far greater than you or I can imagine. It's a leap really, and the fear tries to keep you from taking that leap because "The Lord's not really going to catch you." That is a lie. The Lord has caught me every time, with every leap of faith. With every small first or fiftieth step. Jesus will catch you, and the landing might look rough, but it's like landing in a cloud made of the fluffiest pillows ever created.

Yes, Jesus, the Holy Spirit, and God are gentlemen, but when you are a child of God, he won't stop, just like a parent, just because you said no. He gave me time and experiences between asking for my junk drawer, but eventually I had to say yes. I want you to say yes a lot sooner than I did.

I don't want you to allow the turmoil to try and eat you alive. I want you to find true contentment, healing, wholeness, and completeness in Jesus without all the drama. I want you to live more alive than you are right now. I want you to go night-night with a heart full of peace to receive your rest for the next day. I want you to wake up refreshed every day with a grateful heart overflowing in gladness and peace. To rest in complete contentment no matter what stage of life you are in right this moment.

I want you to know joy like you have never known before. To know peace like never before. Love on a whole new complete level as never before. My friend, I want you to be complete in Jesus. To know what wholeness looks and feels like with Jesus at the helm of your life. I want you to be overflowing in gratitude. Grateful for everything in your life, including the hard stuff you are facing.

From what I have experienced in the hard parts, I thank Jesus. I thank him because I know the hard yuck of life is a lesson I need to learn and ultimately grow from. I'm grateful for everything Jesus does or allows to occur in my life. Not everything he allows am I thankful for in the moment, but it serves his purpose. Don't get me wrong, I complain just like everyone does, but in the grand scheme of things, I am thankful because Jesus still finds me pleasing. He finds it still necessary to correct me like a father corrects his child, and that affords me the luxury of knowing I am still on His radar. I am still his kid, and nothing can change that knowledge in my heart.

Jesus keeps me humble and focused on him. I want you to wake up in the morning and stretch your hands towards the sky and praise Jesus for one more day, and to cherish the moments of the day with Jesus. I don't want you to live in fear anymore of what the day may bring because you got Jesus and he's got you!

Jesus handcrafted and hand-picked you and set you aside for himself. It pleased him to do that with you. You please him, and I want you to remember that every day. He loves you in spite of all the things you've done or that have happened to you. He loves you. Your picture is on his fridge. He looks at you every day and tells you, "I love you _____. You are my kid, yes, my kid. You are beautiful. You are my loving little one. My beloved." He goes on and on about little bitty you!

Isaiah wrote how the Lord's ways are higher than our ways and His thoughts are higher than our thoughts. Jesus thinks very highly of you. To Jesus, you are somebody. You are the love of his life. The beauty of all of these ashes right here, the love of Jesus. The love Jesus lavishes upon us, there is no question you are his favorite. It's true he loves you and loves spending time with you (see Isaiah 55:9 and Isaiah 61:3 NLT).

I didn't totally get all this until I received the Lord's understanding on contentment. Once I learned true contentment, I realized everything I am sharing with you! I realized I was his favorite, just as you are. How truly loved and cherished I am by Jesus. I want you to grow into the love he has for you. I want you to see Jesus take you to another level with him.

I want you to be able to "count it all Joy," like Paul said in Philippians. I want you to experience all of Jesus every day in your life. Trust him to heal those sores and broken places because on the other side of that hurt, pain, and fear is the most deep level of life I've found to date with Jesus. Jesus is my reason for everything and no matter what, I have Jesus, so I have all that I need. I want that to be your truth statement one day, if it isn't already.

With Jesus, I have all I need.

Reflection Questions

1. Are you hiding from the Holy Spirit? Are you trying to keep things a secret from the Holy Spirit? Are you over hiding? Are you ready to shed some light on things?
2. Are you ready to live in your own skin without anxiety or fear looming in or over you?
3. Are you content? Do you want more from this life?
4. Who has access to you? Are they supposed to be there?
5. Are you growing in the correction of God? Are you complaining more than you're praising and thanking him?

CHAPTER ELEVEN

The Raw and the Real

Proverbs 4:23 NLT: Guard your heart above all else, for it determines the course of your life.

Here are five truths to guard your heart:

1. Jesus loves you. He loved you and picked you when your past was still your future. No matter what, he would have endured the cross for just little ole you (see all four gospels, Numbers 14:17–18, and the majority of Psalms. Well, pretty much the entire Bible).
2. You matter to Jesus, and everything in your life matters to him (Psalms 37:23–24).
3. Jesus is a man with the Highest Character, and we can't even fathom all of it. He will not lie, cheat, steal, or give you a gotcha moment (Numbers 23:19). If Jesus said it, so be it (Isaiah 46:11 and 60:22).
4. Jesus is still in the miracle business. He said these signs and wonders shall follow them that believe (Mark 16:17). Everything Jesus did, I can do because the Holy Spirit abides in me (1 John 3:24 and 4:13).
5. Jesus is the same yesterday, today, and forevermore. This encompasses all five (Hebrews 13:8). Do you perceive it (Isaiah 43:19)?

David in Psalms gets me every time. I love how he is totally open, raw, and real about his life, heart, feelings, and emotions. There is no way his walk with all those afflictions was easy, just as our walks aren't the easiest at times and in certain seasons. What we have to remember is that Jesus is right there with us every step of the way. He is our strong tower, our fortress when we are weak, and our refuge when we need hidden in our safe space (2 Samuel 22:2, 22:33, Psalms 61:3 and 91:2, and Proverbs 18:10).

Jesus cares for us and everything we face. He loves us with an unfailing love and an everlasting love that we'll never fully understand this side of Heaven. It's up to us to trust in the Lord with every aspect of our lives. It's up to us to put everything and every part of us in the Father's hands, because he knows what's best for us. It may not look so good now, but when he's finished with it, it will be glorious, beautiful—even show-stopping comes to mind.

I've just grown through something, and I want to share it with you as my wounds are still fresh. I am a person who values honesty, so I endeavor to be honest with you. When you have a promise from the Lord, that doesn't entitle you to a road of pure bliss, rainbows, candy, and kisses. It is a rough, bumpy, and tiresome road.

Tiresome in the fact that the enemy does not want you to get to the promises. He will fight you tooth and nail to keep you from those beautiful promises from the Lord. He will try to break you and beat you down and keep you feeling hopeless and defeated.

Rough in the way trials and afflictions come on you. You are going to get beat up on this road. That is a fact. God allows this to build your faith and trust in him. It is a purifying exercise (Titus 2:14 and Zechariah 13:9). What the devil meant for harm, Jesus, through the Holy Spirit, is going to use it for your good and his Glory.

Bumpy because of the potholes and speedbumps that hinder your progress forward causing you to stumble or give up. The enemy will do anything he can to try and stop you. The operative word there is *try*. He will only succeed if you allow those bumps to stop you and cause you to give in and quit. Do *not*, I repeat, *do not* quit. Don't allow the enemy to win. You know you are guaranteed victory in Christ Jesus. I say to you *push*. Keep *pushing* past the adversary. Victory is mine in Christ Jesus.

It is written the enemy is out to kill, steal, and destroy, but God said he came that we may have life and life more abundantly (John 10:10). The enemy wants to stop you at every turn because he knows if you get to where Jesus is leading you, the enemy gets slapped back off God's kids. He knows you will defeat him. That's why he tries to stop you. He lost already when Jesus took on the cross. Just saying. That's why you fight with prayer and worship to come to the promise and then keep going.

I was given a promise in 2014 of my husband. Here we are in 2018, and I have been struggling for three days with this and wondering if I had lost my ever-lovin' mind. Wondering if I heard wrong that September day all those years ago. I needed to seek the Lord. I needed his word and light on the subject.

The last three days I've been fighting. Fighting for my sound mind. It is written God did not give us a spirit of fear or timidity, but of power, love, and a sound mind (2 Timothy 1:7). Here I was for three days not sleeping well at all, my spirit was not at peace, and I couldn't really eat or sit still for that matter. I was angry at the inner turmoil I was battling. I wanted my Jesus peace, the peace that only God can give, and it truly does surpass all human abilities to understand. I wanted my sound mind back. I wanted my resting posture back. I wanted to hear the Lord but couldn't shut off the noise. The noise of the enemy's stupid whisperings.

Today, on the third day, I got up, Bible in hand, and I headed for my kitchen table. I needed a word. Flat-out, I needed Jesus. I began in Psalms 37 and continued from there. Finally, we are reaching the wee hours of the morning of day four, and I am finally quiet, at peace and rest. I sought the Lord and finally heard him speaking into my heart his words and will for my life.

Finally. Finally, I perceive it. Finally, I know what is going on. If you notice this, the enemy wants nothing good for you. If you are on hell's radar, you can expect a rough road for a little bit, but it is up to us to take our battle stance in our whole armor of God (Ephesians 6:11–18). We must not back down, give in, or run from the battle.

You don't want to get two steps from the top of the mountain and give up. See it to the finish. Don't stop, keep pushing. Push until you see that promise come to pass. (Side note, you do not bring the promise to pass, but God does through you. It is your job to stand in faith trusting and believing in God's ability to do the impossible. We see no way, but he makes a way). It will break forth in a second. Trust the Holy Spirit to guide you through everything. He knows your end from the beginning. Trust him to lead you, guide you, and help you conquer anything that is coming against you and your promises.

The last three days I was told I was basically a waste of human life. I wasn't smart enough. Pretty enough. Good enough. Knowledgeable enough. No life experience. Not intelligent. Not worthy of love. Not valuable to the Lord in any way. Not cherished. My future husband would never pick me. You are useless. You are nothing but a waste of flesh and space. This was on a constant repeat cycle with literally seconds of quiet, but not nearly long enough to hear the Lord Jesus.

Here I sit at 2:30 AM, and I have a word from the Lord. He lit up every lie and burned it off me. Jesus lit up every possible shadow or hiding place the enemy was using to come at me. Then Jesus began to speak into my heart of the promises he's spoken over me, my future, and my family to come. He built that trust up in a matter of minutes. The Holy Spirit knocked down the walls that were trying to encapsulate me. Jesus helped me feel his presence as he consoled me. Jesus is encouraging me to stay in my battle stance and keep my armor on.

To stand firm in and on my foundation, he solidified in me long ago. To trust in his timing (Isaiah 60:22). To trust in his character (Numbers 23:19). To trust that what he speaks over us and in us is going to come to pass, in his time. I cannot rush him or myself in this process because it takes the time it takes. I just have to believe, receive, and trust in Jesus. The Holy Spirit doesn't operate on his own, he only speaks what the Father tells him to speak to us. Just like Jesus (throughout the four gospels: Matthew, Mark, Luke, and John) when he was on the earth. He only did what the Father did.

John 5:19–20 NLT: So Jesus explained, "I tell you the truth, the Son can do nothing by himself. He does only what he sees the

Father doing. Whatever the Father does, the Son also does. For the Father loves the Son and shows him everything he is doing. In fact, the Father will show him how to do even greater works than healing this man. Then you will truly be astonished."

Through all of this, I thought I was walking away from God. Leaving my Father to do it my own way because I was truly done. I had hit my limit, yet every day I still got up and fought—poorly, I know—but nonetheless, I did what I was able to do with the lack of peace, sleep, and food. By food, I mean spiritual and physical food. These bodies, I like to call them our machines, need both types of food. You really can't operate or function properly without either one. I was really running low on fuel.

I thought I was a failure and a huge disappointment to God. I felt like I let him down because I was having trouble fighting for what I want and what he promised me. I thought for a moment there I had lost. That I was defeated. I almost began to believe the lies of the enemy. But God. Oh, but God. He helped me quiet the noise and the nonsense. He said, "Peace, be still, my child." He said, "Enough is enough." At that very moment, Jesus GOT TAPPED IN TO THE RING! Look out. I think Jesus is standing there just waiting and chomping at the bit to get tapped in. He wants to fight your battles. We have to remember that he does, but we just have to tap him in and stand back and let him do what he does best. We have to stand and see the salvation of the Lord. We have to trust that he is fighting for us. We have to trust that there are far more for us than against us (Romans 8:31–33). That's what the enemy wants, to mess with the King's kids and try his hardest to beat us; however, we have an ace up our sleeve, we have the King on our side. When he messes with us, he's going to have to answer to the King himself for messing with the King's kids.

I couldn't praise through this battle. I had to pray through this battle. There is a solid difference, but both are effective. They are atmosphere changing. They are both important. The prayer for me through all of this was just literally speaking the word of God over everything. The word we store up in our hearts that can be pulled out of us in a matter of seconds makes the difference.

Through all of this, the enemy tried to steal not only my promise, my praise, but my voice. My weapon of mass destruction. My voice and my word that is sharper than a two-edged sword (Hebrews 4:12). The Bible says it can separate bone from marrow. That's impeccable and magnificent. The word of God is sharp and fierce.

God used my best friend in all of this mess. He uses everything to help us. She is someone I trust, value, and am so very grateful to have in my life. She is someone who God uses in my life in some of my visions or dreams to depict himself because he knows I trust her. A few years ago, he gave me a dream in the middle of the night. She was sitting at this old metal gray desk and in a wheeled chair that squeaked any time she moved. In this dream, there was a man shrouded in darkness, and the man God promised me illuminated in this hyper bright light. She's looking at me in this dream and keeps asking the same question over and over and over with very little pause between. She asks, "Are you going to settle?" Never raising her voice or getting angry with me but causing me to think and ponder this question deeply in what seems like seconds. I finally stand up and yell, "No, I WILL NOT SETTLE." She pointed at me with a huge smile on her face and pride in her voice and says, "Now that's my girl!"

I tell you this dream to let you in on a secret. This dream kept playing over and over in the pauses for the last three days. That kept giving me hope through all of this that felt like hell and war. The secret is that the answer never wavered. I will not settle in life anymore once the Lord asked me that question and I answered. I am a person of my word. I also kept hearing my pastor's voice, "What God put your name on no other man shall have. They may get there first, but they cannot have your promises."

I kept trying. I kept up with what I could do and tried my best to trust in Jesus. I felt myself taking my focus off Jesus and putting it on the lies. That distraction was enough of an open door that I allowed the enemy to run amok in my sound mind. The enemy did not miss out on that open opportunity I somehow freely gave out. He tried to get me to misfire. He tried to get me so beat up, bloodied, and depressed that I would walk away from the Lord.

I spent pretty much my entire day in the Bible. Locked away in my safe place, taking refuge in the wings of the Lord. This morning he spoke his truth over me and through me once again. He comforted me in my time of need. He opened my eyes to the truths that I hold on to dearly (see the five points at the beginning of this chapter).

Something new the Lord did do with me was sitting me down and had me list out the "problems" one by one. He had me list out the answers from my cheat sheet. Guess what? The answers were greater in number than the problem itself. Writing all that down helped my fix my eyes back on the Lord. It helped me visualize the answer.

The cheat sheet is easy to create. You create it by reading your Bible and storing up that word in your heart and mind. Every test is open book. Every question and every problem we face has an answer. It's simple really. Trust in Jesus, read your Bible, and store up those truths in your heart. Or as Solomon wrote in Proverbs three, wear them as a necklace.

I was ready to quit and throw in the towel and be done. Like that would fix it or something. That's not going to fix anything. All that is going to do is cause even more trouble. That would be all the should-have, could-have, would-haves we experience in life at certain moments and time. The "unanswerable" questions. This girl hates those questions. They eat at you and nag at you to try and drive a sane person to the insane side of life. We are given a sound mind.

I've learned in this raw moment, after this has been settled in my spirit and flesh, that everything in my life matters to God (again, see the five bullet points at the beginning of this chapter). Today he proved that again and provided me with the peace I was seeking from him. I did seek the Lord and his word. I did what was right in this little bump in the road. I felt like a complete and utter failure, but in all honesty, I was winning and succeeding, but I just didn't know it at the time. I was overcoming and conquering. I was standing on my foundation and the word of God to see this come to pass. Trusting in Jesus even though it didn't feel like it. I didn't feel the presence of the Lord for almost three days, which is unheard of for me, which caused me to think I was getting off the path that the Lord placed me on long ago.

All of this was leading up to the moment that I got totally and unequivocally at the end of me. That's where Jesus gets tapped into the ring and takes over. That's where hell knew it was done messing with me. That moment the enemy saw my daddy Jesus step in the ring and tapped me out and took over the situation, the enemy knew he was rendered defeated, helpless, and completely hopeless. You don't mess with the lion and not get the Roar of victory. VICTORY is mine, saith the Lord.

My flesh wanted to quit, run, and hide, but not my spirit. My spirit is connected to my daddy Jesus, and that is where my help comes from. My spirit fought for me. My spirit remained at rest and trust even though my flesh did not. My spirit was running the show, but my flesh was fighting and fighting hard against it because it was not wanting to stay submitted. The battle of spirit versus flesh is off and on. A love/hate relationship if you will.

The double minded moments rob us of our joy, love, and peace (James 1:5–6). It robs us of our precious time. It robs us of the little moments that are there for us to make memories. It can steal all of you in a matter of a moment. I understand on a new level of the scripture that says renew your mind daily (Psalms 94:19, 2 Corinthians 4:16, Ephesians 4:23–24). In this moment, I could not accomplish that on my own. I needed help to renew my mind. I made myself sit and read my Bible yesterday. I didn't want to. I wanted to run and hide, but that just won't do for me.

I wanted to fight, but I was already in a lacking phase. I wasn't diving into my word like I should have been. I wasn't feeding my spirit, and when I am at that point, it never fails, the enemy tries his nonsense. One would think you would learn the lesson that's hidden in the lesson. I know I can be dense and stubborn, but come on, Sara, learn this thing already.

I have learned over time from my pastor that when you are tired and hitting the beginning stages of unrest is when the enemy attacks. He sees an opening; it may be small, but it's there. He never hesitates. God says in Deuteronomy 31:6 that he will never leave us or forsake us. He's right there with us. I kept hearing this roar inside of me. I can only describe it as a lion on super surround sound, on full volume, roaring inside of me. Our spirits are more powerful than we realize. If we listen to our spirit, we will know what is going on and what's to come because it is connected to Jesus, like a child to its mother in the womb.

This is what the Lord said about all of this. I didn't realize this was more so a test than a battle. What a glorious "aha" moment from and with God. God said, "This is how it is going down. This is a pivotal moment in your life and mine. This is the season of change. The beginning of a new thing."

I am at the end of preparation and at the beginning of a new thing. All of this has brought on labor pains. Jesus has to birth the new thing he has for you, through you. It hurts, like when a mother is giving birth (I know it's not the same), but these labor pains are in the spirit. These new things he's doing for you, your promises, have to come from him, through you, to come to pass. He puts you through these seasons of growth to equip you, but at some point, the educational season comes to an end, and the living it out in real time begins.

When he opens up a new door that you could not open before, just know you weren't ready. Now you are equipped to handle that leg of the journey. Now you can go out and help others in a new way, on a new scale, at a new level, in a new season.

Now is when your ministry starts. Now that new business opens and soars. Now that new project you have been daydreaming about can begin to rise out of you. Through the labor pains, we birth the new season of blessings. Not just blessings for us, but being able to bless others, or mentor others, coaching others. You have been tagged in the game, no longer a bench warmer, with preparation. You will "score" many points, so to speak, for the Lord. Now you get to put to use all the things you've grown through. Now you get to help this Kingdom and our King reach others no one but you can reach. Now you really get to work with the Lord in a very new and exciting way.

You have to remember what you learned. Remember the hard parts, for they taught you new ways of thinking, new ways of doing things, new ways in hearing the Lord's will for the day and your life, and new ways to reach the broken-hearted. New ways to reach the lost. New ways to equip others. New ways to praise and worship. New ways to do pretty much everything in your life. The Lord did all of that in your life. The Lord did all of that in you to reach out to his other kids that need you and what you've grown through.

Kids that maybe don't even know him yet, or maybe those kiddos need a helping hand up, that says I know exactly where you are because I, too, was there, and this is where my "but God" moment happened. Those are divine moments with, and for, the Lord. Those are the moments he planned out for you to walk in and be his hands and feet in this world. The moment Matthew twenty-five plays out in the world, but on the big screen in Heaven. In those moments, Heaven is backing you up. In those moments, we are making a way, when we are working for the Lord, because he's working through us.

He wants all his kids to know he's got their backs. Every step you take, the Holy Spirit is right there with you. Allow him to lead you through this new thing just as you allowed him to lead you through the valley, the broken places, and the hurting places. You have become the new creation Paul is talking about in 2 Corinthians. Put away the old and put on the new creation. Isaiah said, "Do you perceive the new thing I am doing?"

Romans 12:2 NLT: Don't copy the behavior and customs of this world, but let God transform you into a new person by changing the way you think. Then you will learn to know God's will for you, which is good and pleasing and perfect.

All the way through the Bible, you see stories of setbacks for comebacks. You have experienced the setbacks, and now is the time for your comeback, kid! It's opening season for the comebacks, the raise-ups, the lift-ups, and the *new*. It's time.

I may be wounded at the moment, but I am far from crushed, smashed, or broken. I am whole. I am a fighter. I am a conqueror. I am victorious. I am an overcomer. I am a KING'S KID.

This chapter is different on purpose. It is set up to help you stand your ground in your whole armor. Knowing and trusting in the Lord even though it is a mess, but know the Lord has you covered on all sides. You also know that you are the winner. Stay the course, trust the Lord and his process in and with your life. He will not ever let you fail so bad you can't stand back up and go again. Trust me, I know, as you can see. We may fall, but it's how we get back up that matters. I love you, and keep pushing to and for your victory in Jesus!

Reflection Questions

1. Are you being honest with God? Are you being honest with yourself?
2. Are you at peace? Are you resting in God? Are you restless? Is your mind sound? Are you tuning into the enemy's whispers or God's words in your heart?
3. Are you perceiving the new thing's God's doing in you? Are you seeing what the Lord's trying to teach you?
4. Are you trying to do it in yourself? Where'd your trust go? Do you need to build on trust? Are you letting Jesus fight your battles?
5. What's stored in your heart? Is it God's word or the enemy's lies?
6. Are you cheating on an open-book exam?
7. Are you finally at the end of you?
8. Are you being double-minded? Is your flesh trying to get you to go against the spirit?

CHAPTER TWELVE

The Human Condition

"Per Jesus, the human condition is not something you can unpack in a short amount of time." It takes time to learn and takes even longer to unlearn all the bad habits he did not intend for us to carry on our own. It takes time to relearn his ways because they are higher than our ways (Isaiah 55:9).

Fear masquerades as anger. Pain masquerades as hurt and offense. Addiction masquerades as perfection. Through the Holy Spirit, all of these can be turned around because Christ Jesus sets us free. Whom the son sets free is free indeed. Stop living behind the mask of perfection and start living the life Jesus gave you. (Addiction here can really be anything. Anything that keeps your focus.)

Be bold enough to step out in faith to live your life Jesus created you to live. Live without fear of rejection of the Lord. He loves you with an everlasting love. He loves you with an unfailing love. In Christ Jesus, we are made whole and righteous. Never doubt that for a second.

Don't allow the enemy to cause you fear of walking in your birthrights as a son or daughter of the Lord Jesus Christ. Never allow fear, pain, offences, or perfection to keep you from the Lord. Fear tells you lies, but so does pain, being offended, and thinking you have to be perfect to come to Jesus.

Let's face facts. *No one* is, or ever will be, on this earth, perfect. No one is, or will be. They think they are, but in all honesty, they are hiding in the darkness. There was only one person that was perfect and knew no sin, and his name is Jesus. We are to live like he did, but he knew we would fall short and fail regularly. He doesn't expect us to be perfect because he knows what it is to be human. In fact, the only way we are perfect is through Jesus (Galatians 2:16 and Ephesians 1:4).

Ecclesiastes 7:20 NLT: There is not a single person in all the earth who is always good and never sins.

Perfection is an unattainable goal you need to strip off yourself immediately. Set realistic goals for yourself with the help of the Holy Spirit. He will lead, guide, and help you achieve them. He will help you achieve every goal, quicker and bigger than you anticipated.

Perfection is a dream killer. The reason why perfection is a dream and goal killer is because it is unattainable. It kills dreams because it's never going to be perfect in regards to finances or timing. It's going to look a lot like work and continual work. You have to remember you can't do it all alone.

You don't have twelve arms, six legs, and twenty-four hands. If you do, please rethink your schedule because you may need to tone it back a bit. I'm just saying. You can only do one thing at a time and do it well. When we multitask too many things, we end up messing one or several of those tasks up, or they aren't our best work. Slow down and take your time. There isn't anything worth losing your mind over. Nothing is worth that, nothing. Take your time, complete one task well, and move on to the next one.

That to-do list is a hindrance. To-do lists get in the way of our divine appointments, occasionally. You can't be too busy for God. Does the stove need cleaned? Of course, but your neighbor's newborn won't sleep, and Mom needs a minute of peace. A minute to collect herself. The stove will keep. Run next door and give her that moment because that's what is most important. Jesus' other two kids next door, Mommy and baby, need a minute. They need you to keep that divine appointment.

One of the beautiful things about the Holy Spirit leading us and guiding us is that he helps us keep those divine appointments. He clearly points them out, whether it be the still small voice in your spirit or you looking out the kitchen window and seeing your neighbor struggling to mow the lawn because he just had back surgery. We never truly understand what someone else is battling unless we open a line of communication. That's what some of those divine appointments are for, for you to step in and lend a helping hand. It's not always about money. It's seriously just your time, your intelligence, and willingness to step up and make a difference. It is something the Lord carved out just for you to do. No one else can because it was all set up, for you.

Those divine appointments get you connected to a person for a moment in time, a season, or a lifetime. We never know, but what we need to do is stay connected to the Lord through his word and prayer.

The lies of perfection and the never-ending to-do list is a true dream and goal killer. Stop waiting on perfection when it comes to time and finances. It's never going to be perfect. Stop waiting for that endless to-do list to be completed before you help the neighbor mow. You don't have to fall into that trap anymore. Whom the son sets free is free indeed.

Fear, worry, and doubt are part of the human condition that Adam and Eve brought upon us when they stepped away from God and ate of the tree of the knowledge of good and evil. We were never meant to carry these burdens. That's why the burden Jesus talks about in Matthew eleven, he says to give it to him. To yoke ourselves to him and that what he gives us is light and easy to carry. They were never to be a part of us. We are to give those cares to him and carry his, Jesus', cares. That's what he's taught us throughout his word, to care for his people, to lend a helping hand.

That means going out of our way and putting our to-do list on hold. Someone else needs us for a minute. Someone needs the helping hand of the Lord and that comes through us. The Lord uses us all in very unique ways. I think that's why Matthew twenty-five sticks out so much in my mind so often. You gave me food, drink, clothing, and you visited me when I was sick and prayed for me. We, in those amazing moments, are truly giving back to God more than we realize.

Matthew 25:34–36 NLT: "Then the King will say to those on his right, 'Come, you who are blessed by my Father, inherit the Kingdom prepared for you from the creation of the world. For I was hungry, and you fed me. I was thirsty, and you gave me a drink. I was a stranger, and you invited me into your home. I was naked, and you gave me clothing. I was sick, and you cared for me. I was in prison, and you visited me.'

We are operating in his ordained divine moments he's scheduled for us. In those moments, we are the hands and feet of Jesus. We are doing exactly what he needs us to do in those moments. After you have completed that divine moment, your to-do list will get done quicker than anticipated because you have been energized by the Holy Spirit. Don't turn people down when they offer a helping hand to you because that just may be your answer to prayer. You never know how God will use you as a divine appointment for someone else's schedule.

He uses us all every day. It could be just a simple hello or a smile to let them know you see them, or it may be a word that he gives you for someone. It could even be a simple hug. That's happened to me before. You get caught up talking, and the Spirit moves, and the next thing you know, you are hugging a stranger in public on aisle five at the grocery store. We never know what God is going to do next, but what I can tell you is that he will show up every day in some way to let you know you are seen and you are loved. Just be ready to jump when he shows you a place to minister to one of his other kids.

Don't be afraid to look foolish. In Corinthians, the Lord had Paul write, "He uses the foolish things to confound the wise" (1 Corinthians 1:27 KJV). People won't always understand because their prayers aren't being answered in the conventional ways of the past. The simple fact is that you are in a new place with new experiences and tests to grow through. Nothing is going to look like it did in the past because you have raised up to a new place. It's all new on this new level. You've grown *to* the new level, now it's time to grow *in* the new level.

Our most important job is to trust Jesus, read our Bible, and believe what he tells us. Fully and openly trust that he will not lead you away from him. If you hear something that goes against God's word, run in the opposite direction. Everything the Lord speaks will always line up with the word of God in the Bible. God will never bait you either. He is for you (Romans 8). There is none of this "Lookie, lookie, here it is, nope, wait, you can't have that I was just joking." No, the Holy Spirit doesn't do that. With the Lord, it's always "I'm going to give you 'XYZ,'" but you have to wait." "XYZ" could be anything under the sun in your life.

The wait may be long, but trust he will bring it to pass in his perfect time (Isaiah 46:11). It always comes back to trust. Trusting in the Lord. The trust exercises kind of suck. They really do, because it's like when your parents say or used to say _____ (fill in the blank), and you'd roll your eyes like "I know." At that moment, your parents trust you until you accidently burn the kitchen floor with flaming spaghetti. I did that, purely accidental though. My parents kind of limited me after that, but it was worse when I missed curfew. I spent time building their trust up in me to only fall and miss it again, but they kept helping me do better and be better.

Jesus is the same way. He is always stretching our faith and trust in him. He's always trying to grow and strengthen your trust in him and in you. Each new season and level requires more trust and faith. The word says, "To whom much is given much is required" (Luke 12:48b). Which means we must grow in every area before we move up to the next level. The good news is he, Jesus, is always right there with us, never leaving us or forsaking us (Deuteronomy 31:6). Trust and believe that now more than ever before in your life. When the enemy, the dirty little liar, tries to whisper in your ear that you are totally alone. My friend, you are never alone. The Holy Spirit will seem quiet when the noise is surrounding you, but as soon as you get to your quiet place, he'll let you know what's going on.

The plus side is that if you can't get quiet, he will have someone come to you and give you his words. That's happened to me before, giving his word to another, and I have also received his word from someone else. He will not hesitate to get you his word. He will send you all the backup you need to do what he's spoken in you to do.

Someone, somewhere, is standing in the gap for you, interceding on your behalf. God's got this.

You will not miss your scheduled divine moments from God. The Lord will not let you miss them. He may just bring them to you. You never know how, but it just happens. It may be at a gas station, school, work, or in your neighborhood and community. He's moving on your behalf, even though you don't see it. He cares for you.

Throw off perfection. Perfection is a dream and goal killer. It will tie you up in so many knots, you can't escape them. It can paralyze you in a season God doesn't want you in anymore. It's time for you to move because the door is open to you; but you have this perfect picture in your head, and that door looks nothing like that picture. It's not going to always look like what you imagined. Ephesians 3:20, "He will do exceedingly abundantly above all we can think, ask or imagine." It's not going to be that perfect picture from your head, but it will be God's perfect version and picture for you.

1 John 4:18 NLT: Fear is crippling, but Perfect love casts out all fear.

Here's the deeper point on trust. We put our trust in people more so than God. I simply think that's because we see people and somewhat know their capabilities; however, we've never seen God, and we don't, nor can we, comprehend what God is totally and completely capable to do. All we really know is that nothing is impossible for God. We put our unattainable expectations on humans, the people we see, and give God the "easy and small" stuff. Give God the big stuff, too. Quit putting these unattainable goals and expectations on people who are never going to fully satisfy you and will never truly accomplish everything you put on them because we are broken. We are not capable of handling God-sized things, but God is able to handle it all.

There are only three answers to our prayers: yes, no, and not yet. "Not yets" are the waiting rooms of life. They are not to cause you harm, but to prepare you and get you ready for the "yes." It's how you wait that determines the time, and sometimes it's your perspective.

If your perspective is off, and you're down and negative, you might be in that waiting room a lot longer than intended. A perspective change is necessary. We have to get that God given perspective. The one that says count it all joy (James 1:2). To praise even though everything is falling apart. You say, "Lord, I lost my job today, but I am still going to praise you today in spite of that because Jesus, you are still on the throne." Praise Him when you fall off the wagon of sobriety, not because you fell off the wagon, but because he can help you climb back up. Praise Him when your business fails because he will help you succeed again. Praise Him in the hardest of times. I never thought that was possible.

Let me tell you something. My grandpa passed away in December 2014. I was sad and hurt, but I praised the Lord through it because he lived. We were blessed to have my grandpa ninety some odd years. That's a blessing and a treasure. We were blessed to have him all those years. Did it still hurt? Of course. Did I still grieve? Of course, but the beauty of a perspective change is now I praise through the difficulty. I pray and read my word and seek the Lord more so in the hard moments, which is true for most people. It's when we need his comfort and a solid reminder of his promises. When you are facing a loss of a friend or family member, a relationship, a job, anything really, seek Jesus. He will comfort you and show you some amazing things in his word and in your spirit, and he will help you through your grieving process.

With the mind shift that accompanies the perspective shift, you can see the problems differently. It helps you keep your eyes on Jesus. When my grandpa passed away, I cried hard. I was angry because I saw him and I dancing on the day of my wedding. That hadn't come to pass yet. I wanted that moment with him like so many of my cousins had. I was pretty mad and sad. In that moment, I started talking to Jesus.

The next day, as I am getting ready to go somewhere, who knows where, I had a vision of my grandpa in Heaven dancing with my grandma, who had passed away before I was ever thought of. I only saw her in pictures before this day, but I knew in that vision that it was my grandma. That was a trip. I saw my grandpa wearing this very stunning and beautiful light gray suit with a crisp white button-down shirt and a striped tie. He had his sleeves rolled up and was dancing around like a wild man. My grandma had on this very vivid red dress. I've never seen a red that shade before in person. It was truly the most beautiful red I've ever seen. It was a classic cocktail dress. There my grandparents are in their youth again swing dancing, laughing, and having a gay old time. It was beautiful. They were healthy, happy, and excited to be together again.

In that moment is where the Lord said, "Sara, they are with me. You'll see them again one day not too soon. Don't cry because he died, but be glad and thankful he lived." Immediately, I was at peace. No more sadness and no more worry. His funeral was beautiful with the full military service at the graveside. It was one of the most beautiful things I've seen in my life. These men came out to honor my grandpa. What they did was a blessing.

Even when we lose somebody, we can still be blessed. It's all about aligning your mind to the word of God and God himself, but you do still grieve and cry when you reminisce, just not out of sadness. It's a joy because they lived. It's tears because you loved them and still love them. There is nothing wrong with your tears or your grief. We all grieve differently. Please do not think I am telling you not to grieve. No. You take your time through the grief, but don't get stuck there. Remember they lived. They loved you just as much as you loved them.

I am not telling you my perspective is perfect and always focused on Jesus. Come on, I'm still human. Ha! That would be a total lie, for real. There are times, especially when I am driving, that I'm way off. For example, someone slams on the brakes and turns without a turn signal. In that moment, I have two choices. I can thank the Lord my brakes stopped me, and I didn't hit them; or I can curse them out. Some days I do the first choice, and there are other times I do the latter; but in a moment like that, the correct perspective is to be thankful I didn't hit them and or possibly cause them or myself bodily harm.

The proper perspective leads to the proper posture. The proper posture is to stay at rest in Jesus. To stay at peace in Jesus. To trust Jesus completely. Don't allow the stuff we see or the evil running around in this world get us all up in the air. To stay calm and keep our eyes fixed on Jesus.

Let me explain the "up in the air" posture. We get angry and mad about the enemy running amok, but don't allow it to steal your focus. Don't allow it to steal your joy. We conquer evil by doing good (Romans 12:12). The good we do with our divine appointments and prayer over people is how we conquer evil. We speak the word of Jesus over people fully trusting that the Holy Spirit will uphold the word of God because he never fails to do so (Psalms 5:3 and Romans 8:37).

When we maintain our posture and perspective on and in Jesus, we can actually stay in those two areas properly. Keeping our eyes fixed on Jesus isn't always the thing we want or try to do. It is something we all learn and continue to learn. When our eyes are fixed on Jesus everything lines up. Nothing can stay out of order in our lives when we have our eyes fixed on Jesus. Everything has an order, and if it's out of order start checking yourself. Are your eyes fixed on Jesus? Are you to focused on self? Did you pick up fear and begin to believe its lies, again? Or is it doubt or worry? Is it another person? Or money?

Something is always trying to steal our focus. Once it steals your focus away from Jesus, then it starts throwing everything out of order. After that happens, it feels like you are falling apart. It keeps our focus so long that we even forget about Jesus. It happens. Anyone that tells you otherwise is, in my opinion, lying.

I've known Jesus my whole life, and the relationship status has changed over the years. At the age of twenty-one, our relationship status changed. It went from just my parents covering and salvation over me to my very own salvation over me. I've had long and short terms of seasons where my focus has shifted off him and onto myself. That's when things get a little like a madhouse for me. I lose order, and control follows soon after.

God, in true fashion, gives me a nice little talking to or a nice healthy slap on my booty. He always helps me shift back to him, and it's always followed with repentance and tears on my part. The slap on the bottom is because I have gotten into something I was never meant to be a part of. I told you in a previous chapter about falling out of sobriety. This is not a literal slap, just usually a stern, "*Sara.*"

With God, I know it may be a rocky road from time to time, but I know he's with me through it all. He's educating me through it all. I know he will do the same for you as he has for me. He will illuminate these things in you. He will help you change your posture and your perspective. He will help you fix your eyes on him.

He will bring your spiritual eyes into focus for you. What you have to do is surrender to him all of you (your mind, body, spirit, and soul). Your focus will shift, just give it some time. Start carving out time throughout your day to pray and read your Bible in the quiet spaces. It can be five minutes or five hours. There is not a set time limit, but take that time to spend with the Lord. You will not regret it. In all honesty, you'll be thinking, "Why didn't I do this sooner? Why didn't I start this a while ago?" Just remember, baby steps. You do not have to do what someone else does. You go at your own pace reading and studying because everyone learns differently. Learn at your own pace. The Lord will help you grow your time with him and in the process, you will grow to cherish that time with him. You will protect that time for that study, eventually (Isaiah 30:15).

The longer you study, pray, and spend time in the presence of the Lord, the more you will crave it. Nothing compares to that quiet time. I like to do my quiet time either first thing in the morning or right before bed. It helps me start my day on the right track, and it helps me quiet the noise before I go to sleep. The longer you grow in Jesus, the more intimate your relationship becomes. The relationship between you and Jesus will grow and blossom into something so amazing. That's how I fell in love with Jesus. I know I've already told you all that, but it's worth saying it again. Jesus will help you get your life in line, but you have to trust him to do his part. It always comes back to trust.

Reflection Questions

1. What's telling you that you have to be perfect? What mask are you wearing? What trap of perfection is holding you back? What is trapping you in perfection?

2. What are your goals? Are they realistic for this season or for the future only?

3. What's on your to-do list? Is it overwhelming you? Is it keeping you from living in the moment? Are you missing your divine appointments?

4. Does it scare you to be his hands and feet? Are you afraid they won't allow you to do for them as God's directed you to do? Are you afraid you won't live up to the task at hand?

5. What trust exercises are you experiencing? Do they even look like trust exercises? Does it feel like a never-ending mess with a hopeless resolve?

6. Are you putting unattainable expectations on someone?

7. How's your perspective? Do you see only negativity? How do you view life? How do you view yourself?

8. What posture are you sitting in? Peace? Rest? Anger? Bitterness? Hate? Love?

9. Are you in order or disarray?

CHAPTER THIRTEEN

Salvation: The Road Less Traveled By

Revelation 3:20 KJV: Behold, I stand at the door and knock: if any man hear my voice, and open the door, I will come in to him and will sup with him, and he with me.

This scripture caught my eye a while ago. It was a scripture I had heard for months, from people randomly around me, leading up to the day I asked Jesus into my heart. Today I want to share it with you and how the Holy Spirit showed me this in a vision. The Holy Spirit is pretty cool.

The Lord showed me this. He rings your bell at your house. You're all like "Okay, I'm coming." He rings the bell again. Again you say, "I'm coming." At one point, he starts ringing that doorbell without stopping. Finally, you get annoyed and fling that door open. When you open the door you think, "Great, it's a solicitor trying to get me to buy into the stuff they are selling," but Jesus says, "I'm not selling you anything. I am here to give you this free gift of life and life more abundantly [John 10:10]. No purchase necessary. Just a free gift every day that has a daily supply value of grace, mercy, forgiveness, love, joy, happiness, compassion, and peace [Galatians 5:1–26]."

Then you're all like "But the house isn't clean, and the dishes are piled up. Laundry is everywhere, and for the life of me, I can't find the source of the stink." Jesus says, "I really don't care that it's a mess, because I've come to clean it up and out." Jesus is all like "I'm a housekeeper. I am here to help you take care of all this." Jesus says, "I'm the way, the truth, and life, nobody comes to the father except through me." There is a choice, but it's simple: do you let Jesus in the house, or do you keep him at arm's length on the porch? It's that simple. I say let him in the house.

Jesus died on the cross and rose three days later for you to have a life worth having and an eternity with him in Heaven. See all four gospels: Matthew, Mark, Luke, and John. All four have the accounts of the cross spelled out for you to read, to see what all he endured for you. This man Jesus is the only god to die for his people. The only one to lay his life down and pick it back up so we may have life and life more abundantly. He is the way, the truth, and the life.

The day you choose Jesus, life becomes different (Joshua 24:15). It becomes outstanding, but it becomes hard in some aspects. That's the moment you draw a line in the sand. That's a monumental step in your life. At that moment and from that time forward, the Holy Spirit lives in you. The changes begin to take place, and a lot of those changes you don't even realize are happening in those moments.

The Holy Spirit immediately begins pulling and throwing things off you. Instead of resisting and pushing or pulling away from those changes, I want you, and the Holy Spirit wants you, to lean into him. Lean into those movings and shakings he's doing inside of you.

When the Holy Spirit begins clearing and cleaning his throne off in your heart, he's setting up residence in your heart like the word says, he abides in us so we may abide in him (1 John 2:27–29 KJV). That's the day your new journey begins. The day a huge shift occurs in your life.

A day you'll never forget. A day you will look forward to every day after, to praise the Lord for that glorious day you made a huge change in your life for the better. A chance at true happiness, joy, peace, loving kindness, and an overall satisfaction that you will never be alone for the rest of your life (John 15:15).

You now have a true best friend, a confidant, a partner in hope, a true love that you've never known before. The word calls the Holy Spirit one that sticks closer than a brother (Proverbs 18:24). That's

130

a true statement. Others will come and go, in and out of your life, but the only one that will never ever hurt you, leave you, or stab you in the back is the Holy Spirit. He will never lead you astray. He will never throw you under the bus. He will never say, "Oops, sorry, you're on your own." It will never be like that with Jesus. He will never leave you or forsake you (Deuteronomy 31:6, one of my very most favorites).

It has been my hope to lead you to this point. To either lead you closer to Jesus or help you truly come to know Jesus. Either way, it is win-win! I can't voice this enough; it is truly the best, most amazing, and glorious decision I've ever made. I asked Jesus into my life one faithful day in September 2003. I will never forget that day. I will always rejoice the loudest every year on my spiritual birthday. It's a day I look forward to every year. I like to reminisce with the Lord and all he's done in my life since that day. I find that is the most appropriate day to do that with him.

It's funny, as I write this chapter, that day is very near to my mind, my heart, and coming up this Sunday. I can't wait for that day, to get up and praise, for it is my birthday. I can't tell you what I was wearing or even the message Benny preached that night, I just knew without a doubt that Jesus was speaking to my heart that day.

When we ask Jesus into our heart, Jesus licks us and yells "MINE!" In my household, this is a running joke and has been for some years now. It goes a little like this: if there is only one piece of pizza or one chicken wing left and you want it, you better lick it and proclaim that it is yours or someone else will; and when you lick it, you have to yell "MINE." In life, that happens, metaphorically speaking, three times: once with your parents when you are born, when you marry your spouse, and the day you meet Jesus and ask him into your heart. That last one is the most important in my life because I love being his! I love that he calls me his daughter. I melted that day he yelled "MINE" when I asked him into my heart all those years ago. I've never felt truly deserving of that love, and I believe most everyone questions how someone could love them that much considering their pasts. The beauty is that Jesus loves us more than we could humanly handle. He suffered the worst death so that we may be free. That we could walk boldly into his presence and his loving arms (Ephesians 3:12).

"Jesus still loved you and picked you when your past was still your future. Let me say it again. When your history was still your future, God loved you" (my pastor, Pastor Ron Carpenter Jr. Redemption Church).

When I heard my pastor utter those words, I had to take a pause to absorb all of what he spoke. That statement knocked my socks off, and I wasn't even wearing socks that day. I couldn't tell you anything else about that service on that Sunday morning because I was dwelling on that statement. I sat and thought about that statement for days. It was getting down in my heart and working itself out. Knowing without a doubt that God never hesitated to pick me no matter what I had done was mind-blowing, and mind you, I had been born again for ten years or better at that moment. I was overflowing in the magnitude of this statement. The love of God just poured out in me. The power of that statement is so massive to me. It speaks volumes to my heart still to this day.

If this message spoke to you and you really hear the Lord ringing your bell trying to get your attention, I am encouraging you to pray the following prayer. I encourage you to take a leap of faith. To take this first step to a new life and a new you. Paul said, "I know it to be true because I've seen the work God's done in me—therefore if any man be in Christ, he is a new creature; old things are passed away, behold all things are become new (2 Corinthians 5:17)." This is what takes place when Jesus steps into your life fully. You become a new creature. Your desires change, outlooks change, hearts are changed, because of the work Jesus is doing inside of you. Trust in Jesus, to help you open the door and gladly welcome Jesus into your heart. To say "Yep, I need help. I need you. I am at the end of me, Jesus." Be bold. Be courageous. Be without fear and boldly pray the prayer I have for you below.

Without further ado, let us pray and ask Jesus into our hearts and/or renew your heart in Jesus if you feel you have backslid or walked away. If you have never asked Jesus into your hearts, here is your chance. It's easy. It's a short prayer. Just read it out loud. Boldly speak this prayer out loud where you are. Don't fear. Jesus is not some mean guy; he loves you.

> *Dear Lord Jesus, I come boldly to you today. Lord Jesus, I am a sinner and I repent of my sins. I believe that you, Jesus, died and rose from the dead three days later. Jesus, I ask that you come into my heart today and wash me clean. I ask that you take your rightful place on the throne of my heart. I ask that you abide in me so I may abide in you. Forgive me, Jesus, for all the mistakes I've made. Renew me now, Jesus. Create in me a heart that is pure, Jesus. Wash me clean with your blood, Jesus. Jesus, today I make you my Lord and savior. In Jesus' name I pray, amen.*

With that simple prayer, I believe you were born again. Now is the time for celebration. You just made Heaven shout with joy and caused a party to erupt. I want you to hear it from me first, "Welcome to the family, baby!" I love you so much. I am so thankful we are related. This family just got blessed with the most amazing and beautiful you, ever! YAY!

Hebrews 10:16–18 NLT: "This is the new covenant I will make with my people on that day, says the Lord: I will put my laws in their hearts so they will understand them, and I will write them on their minds so they will obey them." Then he adds, "I will never again remember their sins and lawless deeds." Now when sins have been forgiven, there is no need to offer any more sacrifices.

Romans 5:1–2 NLT: Therefore, since we have been

> Jesus will meet you right where you are. If you are at rock bottom, he will climb into that pit and help you out and up. He will begin mending you right there. The healing process is on your time frame. It's up to you to choose (Daniel 3:1–30 and Daniel 6:1–24).

made right in God's sight by faith, we have peace with God because of what Jesus Christ our Lord has done for us. Because of our faith, Christ has brought us into this place of highest privilege where we now stand, and we confidently and joyfully look forward to sharing God's glory.

Romans 5:11 NLT: So now we can rejoice in our wonderful new relationship with God—all because of what our Lord Jesus Christ has done for us in making us friends of God.

Romans 5:20–21 KJV: Moreover the law entered, that the offence might abound. But where sin abounded, grace did much more abound: That as sin hath reigned unto death, even so might grace reign through righteousness unto eternal life by Jesus Christ our Lord.

If you want a great read in your Bible, check out Colossians. I read it about a year ago, and it opened my heart and eyes even more to my salvation. Paul wrote Colossians, and it's all about being reconciled to God and about salvation and being born again. It's a wonderful read and study. This book in the Bible really speaks to me on a deeper level than I can completely understand still to this day. Colossians somewhat blows my mind because it speaks about being made right with God and how Jesus sees us as righteous and blameless. We focus on our mistakes, yet God does not, but does see us as holy, righteous, and redeemed. We need to see ourselves all the ways Jesus sees us.

> **I always wondered where all these pastors got this prayer from. One day, I heard the Lord tell me to read Psalms 51. So I did, and here it is for you to see and read. This is what David prayed after he committed adultery and murder. Psalms 51:1–19 NLT: "Have mercy on me, O God, because of your unfailing love. Because of your great compassion, blot out the stain of my sins. Wash me clean from my guilt. Purify me from my sin. For I recognize my shameful deeds—they haunt me day and night. Against**

you, and you alone, have I sinned; I have done what is evil in your sight. You will be proved right in what you say, and your judgement against me is just. For I was born a sinner—yes, from the moment my mother conceived me. But you desire honesty from the heart, so you can teach me to be wise in my inmost being. Purify me from my sins, and I will be clean; wash me, and I will be whiter than snow. Oh, give me back my joy again; you have broken me—now let me rejoice. Don't keep looking at my sins. Remove the stain of my guilt. Create in me a clean heart, O God. Renew a right spirit within me. Do not banish me from your presence, and don't take your Holy Spirit from me. Restore to me again the joy of your salvation, and make me willing to obey you. Then I will teach your ways to sinners, and they will return to you. Forgive me for shedding blood, O God who saves, then I will joyfully sing of your forgiveness. Unseal my lips, O Lord, that I may praise you. You would not be pleased with sacrifices, or I would bring them. If I brought you a burnt offering, you would not accept it. The sacrifice you want is a broken spirit. A broken and repentant heart, O God, you will not despise. Look with favor on Zion and help her; rebuild the walls of Jerusalem. Then you will be pleased with worthy sacrifices and with our whole burnt offerings; and bulls will again be sacrificed on your altar."

I know it may be weird for you to think that Jesus would use that simple prayer to change your life, but he did. He is going to start turning lights on in your heart. He is going to help you start a new adventure and journey with him. He just licked your little beautiful heart and yelled, "Mine!" You are his, baby! You are his beloved child, saved by grace, through faith. Welcome to the family, kid! I am so excited to have you be a part of this amazing, large, loud, and loving family. It's not always easy; but, kid, it's so worth it, and you have more people on your side than you can imagine.

Here are some amazing scriptures I want to share with you as you begin your new journey on this day. I love all of these. They are wonderful to dwell on and remember as often as you can. Start storing up word in your heart. These are excellent starters.

Ephesians 4:5–6 NLT: There is only one Lord, one faith, one baptism, and there is only one God and Father, who is over us all and in us all and living through us all.

Ephesians 2:3 NLT: All of us used to live that way, following the passions and desires of our evil nature. We were born with an evil nature and we were under God's anger just like everyone else.

Ephesians 4:2–3 NLT: Be humble and gentle, be patient with each other, making allowances for each other's faults because of your love. Always keep yourselves united in the Holy Spirit, and bind yourselves together with peace.

Psalms 50:2 NLT: But giving thanks is a sacrifice that truly honors me!

Proverbs 18:10 NLT: the name of the Lord is a strong fortress; the godly run to him and are safe.

Proverbs 18:24 NLT: There are "friends who destroy each other but a real friend sticks closer than a brother."

Psalms 119:105 NLT: Your word is a lamp for my feet a light on my path.

Ephesians 1:17 NLT: I keep asking that the God of our Lord Jesus Christ, the glorious Father, may give you the Spirit of wisdom and revelation, so that you may know him better.

Colossians 3:15 NLT: And let the peace that comes from Christ rule in your hearts. For as members of one body you are all called to live in peace. And always be thankful.

2 Timothy 1:7 NKJV: For God has not given us a spirit of fear, but of power and of love and of a sound mind.

Colossians 1:27 NLT: For it pleased God to tell his people that the riches and glory of Christ are for you Gentiles, too. For this is the secret: Christ lives in you, and this is your assurance that you will share in his glory.

Reflection Questions

1. Is Jesus ringing your bell? Is he asking to join you?
2. Is Jesus offering to help you get your heart right? He's waiting on you, are you ready?
3. Have you drawn your line in the sand? Did you feel the shift? Do you feel lighter?
4. Did you accept Jesus as your Lord and Savior? If so, let me be the first to say it again: "Welcome to the family!" I wish I could hug you right now!

CHAPTER FOURTEEN

Relationship Is More than a Word; It's a Privilege

David tells us this in Psalms 32:1–11 NLT (a psalm of David):

> *Oh, what joy for those whose rebellion is forgiven, whose sin is put out of sight! Yes, what joy for those whose record the Lord has cleared of sin, whose lives are lived in complete honesty!*
>
> *When I refused to confess my sin, I was weak and miserable, and I groaned all day long. Day and night your hand of discipline was heavy on me. My strength evaporated like water in the summer heat. Interlude.*
>
> *Finally, I confessed all my sins to you and stopped trying to hide them. I said to myself, "I will confess my rebellion to the Lord." And you forgave me! All my guilt is gone. Interlude.*
>
> *Therefore, let all the godly confess their rebellion to you while there is time, that they may not drown in the floodwaters of judgement. For you are my hiding place; you protect me from trouble. You surround me with songs of victory. Interlude.*

The Lord says "I will guide you along the best pathway for your life. I will advise you and watch over you. Do not be like a senseless horse or mule that needs a bit and bridle to keep it under control." Interlude.

Many sorrows come to the wicked, but unfailing love surrounds those who trust the Lord. So rejoice in the Lord and be glad, all you who obey him! Shout for joy, all you whose hearts are pure!"

David praised the Lord for his salvation before he ever really sinned. David was a man after God's own heart. He sang praises to the Lord. He danced in the presence of the Lord with his whole body. David truly loved Jesus, and it shows throughout the books of the Bible that speak of David. I think that's why I love David so much. He and I are like two peas in a pod. I love Jesus. I love to sing and dance with Jesus. Jesus is my main squeeze, my main man, my BFF, my everything.

I can tell you this, it is true. The Bible says that the Lord throws our sins as far apart as the east is from the west and chooses to remember them no more (Psalms 103:12 KJV and Hebrews 8:12 KJV). You are going to go through all of this from this day forward in your life. Trust the Lord to work all things together for your good. Trust the Lord to lead you and guide you. Allow the Lord to bring new people into your life to help you in every way possible.

Building a relationship with Jesus is simple and easy. Read your Bible and pray. When you pray, just talk with Jesus like you talk to your best friend. There is no right or wrong way to pray. Prayer is a hotline to God. It's opening your heart up to him and voicing your heart to him. He already knows your heart, but he wants you to be willing to speak it to him. It's a trust thing. It's an open line of communication. In this you must be willing to sit still and wait for the Lord to speak into your heart his truth and will for your life. Be willing to shut all the noise out to be still and quiet to hear him.

The other part of relationship with Jesus is allowing him total access to you, in you, and through you. To allow him to work in you and through you with all the things in your life. To allow him to open up your gifts, disciple you, correct you, grow you, and mature you. All of these come with time spent in the Bible. Time spent in the Bible brings closeness to Jesus. Let me tell you this from my personal experience: take your time and read your Bible slowly. This isn't a race. Start small. One verse a day is okay. Meditate on that one verse until you feel it working in you. Then move up from there. There is no time limit nor a specific amount of time you must spend in your word daily. No. No. Don't set yourself up for that because if you forget then you'll feel guilty because you didn't do your hour reading time. No, just take your time and enjoy your journey.

"*I deliberately carve out time in my prayer life to be still and listen for God's voice*" (Priscilla Shirer, *Discerning the Voice of God. How to Recognize when God Is Speaking*—excellent read by the way).

It's all about the journey with Jesus. It's your journey; no one can live your journey for you, just you. Take your time. Grow in the word. Fall in love with Jesus. It won't take long. I can tell you this: I love reading my Bible. I love that when I unzip my case and the pages of my Bible begin to fall open, I feel peace. As I read, I feel the presence of the Lord begin to surround me and envelop me. One day, you, yourself, will be there. Again, this isn't a race. You don't have to compete for time with Jesus. He's never too busy for you. He's standing there with open arms, waiting for you to come in and partake in the meal with him.

Another thing I wish and desire for you to build your relationship with the Lord Jesus is to get in a good Bible-based church. Get in a church that isn't afraid to truly teach the word of God. Yes, I said it. Some churches will teach it their way instead of God's way. By that, I mean it's full of man-made doctrine. You don't need religion, but what you do need is a true relationship with Jesus. Jesus isn't a religion no matter what some might say. It's truly a relational partnership between you and Jesus. When you finally find your home church, start serving in church. Get a support system surrounding you with those beautiful people, a place you can go and truly get feed the word of God, a place that encourages you to grow and seek the Lord in every area of your life.

Getting in a church is excellent. Finding my home church, finally, after years of searching was actually across the country. It was just relocated to the other side of the great United States, but by the grace of God, I can attend church every weekend via the internet. It was a place I finally felt the Lord's word being taught and not the pastor's view on the scriptures. I finally found what I needed and had been searching for for years. In my spirit, I felt like I was home. I was welcomed with open arms.

I serve in my community. I help where I can. I do what I know in my heart to do for the wonderful people in my community. I might not be able to serve my church family in person, but I can surely serve my Father who art in Heaven right where I am. Through finding my church home, I finally realized what being submitted to God looked like, and what it looked like to hold a servant's heart. Find ways to serve in your community and your church. Do it without expectation of things in return. It is truly something that will bless your heart as you bless others.

Serving helps bring a closeness with the Lord. As you grow with the Lord and learn how to be a servant to your Father, he will guide you to people to help. He will show you right where you need to serve to help him and help

Okay a short vocab lesson. *Submission,* per the dictionary, is the action or fact of accepting or yielding to a superior force or to the will or authority of another person. *Intimacy,* per the dictionary, is close familiarity or friendship, closeness. You will hear these two words in church often. They are not dirty, perverted words as you can see. They are words that are used to describe relationship with Jesus and others. Do not let the enemy twist these two around in your head or your heart.

you to grow and mature. It's beautiful to serve. Not long ago, I had the pleasure to serve my mama. She's been sick here lately, but God is showing off in her life through all of this. Anyway, he allowed me to wash her feet the other day. In that moment of washing her feet, I felt so blessed that I was able to do that for her when she couldn't do it for herself. I feel that same way when I serve the amazing people of my community, and in those moments. I feel so close to the Lord.

In regard to submission, it isn't easy because we have this need to control things. We want to be the ones that say when, but in submission to Jesus, we don't have that. When we take our submitted position in Jesus, he says when. He shows you the next step, what doors to walk through, and when to walk through them. You don't even realize you walked through a door. You just are there, and you do what you know to do because in your seasons of preparation, you were equipped for that very moment.

A relationship with Jesus isn't something I talk about to get attention. It is a privilege to have a relationship with him, knowing that with each passing day, he is pulling me closer to him, growing and helping me take all my baby steps he's ordered.

I can't express this enough: enjoy your journey. Enjoy getting to know Jesus through his word. Enjoy that new relationship with Jesus. He will show you and help you in everything. Just have fun and enjoy this new adventure. Take time to grow and live out all that he is going to build up in you.

I encourage you to read this over yourself as often as you would like. This is something the Lord spoke into my heart around June 2018. It was something I needed to hear. I was in a few days of doubt about my abilities and what I was actually capable of doing. I was questioning if I was educated enough to go forward into my future with the Lord. I was really having trouble. But God...God showed up in my doubt and crushed it like he always does. I hope this encourages you. As you read this over yourself, I know, I just know, it will get into your heart and work itself out in you.

Fill in the blanks with your name.

_____, if you could gain all the knowledge in the world and not have me, Jesus, you would be nothing. With me, you have everything. Knowledge isn't all powerful. The power of knowledge lies in me, Jesus, alone. Knowledge by itself is nothing. Nothing but emptiness, but with me, Jesus, and my knowledge, you are unstoppable. You win every time with me, Jesus, in your corner.

Living your life for me, _____, isn't easy, and I never promised it would be, but I did promise you it would be worth it all. When you have me, Jesus, in your heart, you can do all things. Nothing is unachievable. You can do everything I've called you to do, because I know how to do everything I've called you to do. So take heart for I have overcome the world, and I, Jesus, live in you. You can do everything, every step before you, you can do because I am walking with you at every turn. Be of good cheer, _____, it's time to move on from this place and go to the places I've called you to, doing what I lead you to, and helping who I place before you.

Don't worry, I have everything taken care of for you. Every step of this process has had an educational purpose. So don't get side-tracked thinking you know what's going to happen. In all honesty, you have no clue, truly only I, Jesus, know what will happen in your life. We've seen it from beginning to end with every possibility placed before you. We know the outcome. If you keep the faith, you will see victory after victory with me, Jesus, at the helm. Trust me, my child, you are victorious right now, where you sit. You are victorious because I conquered the grave.

My child, I have you covered on all sides, no part lacking covering. Trust me, my child, I have you in the palm of my hands. Trust me with your life. Surrender it all to me. Let it all go and trust me to handle it for your best interests and my glory. Trust me. Trust me.

I will give you the appropriate amount of rest required for your day tomorrow. Trust me, my child. Keep going. Keep doing what you know I've called you to do. You know deep within your heart the right things to do. Until I tell you otherwise, stay on the course I've charted for you.

You are not a failure, _____. It's not possible for you to be a failure because that is saying I, Jesus, am a failure because I am your author, finisher, and your creator. I Am is not a failure, and neither are you, _____.
You are a beautiful masterpiece, because I created you. I made you. I formed you. You are a perfect design. You are my child, _____.

Trust me, my child, no harm shall befall you or your family. Trust me, my child, you are covered by me, Jesus, safe in my arms, hidden from the enemy. You are my beloved, _____. Remember that every day, my love. You, _____, are my beloved child. I love you, my child, far more than you can fathom this side of Heaven. Trust me, my child. Trust me.

Love,
Your Daddy Jesus.

Proverbs 3:13–20: Happy is the person who finds wisdom and gains understanding. For the profit of wisdom is better than silver, and her wages better than gold. Wisdom is more precious than rubies; nothing you desire can compare with her. She offers you life in her right hand, and riches and honor in her left. She will guide you down delightful paths; all her ways are satisfying. Wisdom is a tree of life to those who embrace her; happy are those who hold her tightly. By wisdom the Lord founded the earth; by understanding he established the Heavens. By his knowledge the deep fountains of the earth burst forth, and the clouds poured down rain.

Jesus spoke this into my heart when I needed it most. I am so very thankful I wrote it down so I could go back and read over it as often as I like. I need this reminder from time to time. All of this the Lord spoke into my heart that night was so important at that moment; however I didn't realize how important until today. He gave me this beautiful word to give to each one of you. To encourage each one of us on those days when doubt, worry, fear, failure, and nothingness tries to sneak in. In those times when we need a word from God, he's there for us. I told you earlier in the book that God would show you every day how much he loves you, and when he gave me this gem, he was showing me in my time of need how much he loved me, and that flows down to you.

We reap the benefits of other's obedience from time to time, and this is one of those moments. The Lord taught me in 2014 to write it down when he begins to speak in my heart. Since then, I write down pretty much everything I hear in my heart when he speaks. I encourage you to do the same when you hear that still small voice of the Lord beginning to speak in you. It truly helps me. I write so much, whether it is a text to myself or in a notebook. It really helps to come back to that word in an hour when you can't get quiet. I encourage you to trust in the Lord. I promise he will not lead you down a path he didn't equip you for.

Reflection Questions

1. Are you shutting out the unwanted noise? Are you sitting still and listening?
2. Are you looking for an opening to serve in your community?
3. Are you being show what it looks like to truly be submitted to God? How to surrender completely?
4. Are you being taught the word of God?

FINAL THOUGHTS

- Study your Bible daily to build a relationship with Jesus.
- Allow God's love to blossom and bloom in your heart and overflow out of you to others.
- Trust God to work all things together for your good and his glory in your life.
- Don't put time limits on God.
- Take God out of the box.
- Lean into God and acknowledge him in all your ways.
- The steps of a righteous man are ordered. Walk in your steps he's carve out just for you.
- Stay the course with the Lord.
- The Lord will never let you fail so bad you can't stand back up and go again.
- We may fall, but it's how we get back up that matters.
- A relationship with Jesus isn't a race. It's not a sprint. It's a marathon.

CONCLUSION

This is my story of how I fell in love with Jesus. This journey started for me at twenty-one years old. It took me about nine years to cultivate this relationship with Jesus to where I would fully begin to open up to him freely. When I turned twenty-nine, my prayer life changed a great deal. By the time I turned thirty-one and started my college years with Jesus, I didn't realize how quickly I would fall in love with him. I fell in love with my Lord and Savior. I never knew that was a possibility for me. God showed up in the middle and started speaking to my heart in a way I had only dreamed about, some day off in the future. The Lord did not hesitate to pull me into him. He did not hesitate to love me or call me his. I was slow to take that major leap of faith. I pray you don't take that long. I pray you start leaning into him now.

I had the revelation of this first chapter in March of 2016. It wasn't until November of 2016 that I finally sat down and began to write out what turns out to be this beautiful book. All the while, I was thinking that this was a sermon, or a series of sermons. Wow, how funny I was to believe so little from my Lord. He does things so much grander and greater than we can ever ask, think, or imagine.

It was easy to write this book because the Holy Spirit gave me every word, line, and paragraph. The hard part was battling the negative thoughts. The thoughts that say *This is a waste of your time. No one will read this book. No one will understand your thoughts or thought process. Nobody cares about your journey.*

That's simply not true. If it wasn't something God wanted done in my life, through my life, or with my life, he would have never pulled all of this out of me. He would have never given me this life or path to walk. I know this will change lives and it will have an impact on the Kingdom of God. I just know it to be true.

My story is my own, and I am the only one that can tell the story. I will say I am thankful for the journey thus far, because if I hadn't taken it, I would not be the person God designed me to be.

I love myself and the woman God himself is creating me to be. She is beautiful, magnificent, and breathtaking. It sounds like I am stuck on myself falling into the trap of vanity, but in all honesty, I finally saw and see myself through Jesus' eyes. I finally saw what all the fuss was, and is, about.

Writing this book showed me my bigger picture and grew me even more. It ministered to my heart along the way. God used my own story to encourage me and bless me at the same time. He knew that to be real with everyone also meant I had to be real with myself and him. I had to unpack some more bags. I had to really be willing to let pretty much all of me out and place it all on the table for all to see. It's not easy always doing that, but transparency is very important, in my opinion. I am not ashamed of my past. I don't regret my past. I don't want anyone to think I am bragging on my past either. I don't regret much, nor am I embarrassed easily. I'm just not designed that way.

This is really only parts of me. God didn't give out all of my life because he respects our privacy just as much as we ourselves should. He used the important parts to educate others. Please don't walk your path the hard way, like I have. Know that walking with Jesus is not easy and there are bumps, and hills, and valleys, and beautiful mountain tops along the way you will have to walk. Trust the journey, and you will see the amazing story one day that God is writing in you, through you, and with you. It's a beautiful story!

What a journey so far. I can't wait to see what else Jesus does in my life. I know it won't be perfect, but it will be perfect for me. I love you! Jesus loves you! Remember that always!

SCRIPTURE REFERENCE

I have all of these scriptures listed out in this format so you can take your time and study as you like. This way, they are all in one location, and you don't have to write them down as you go. I want to be as helpful and encouraging as possible. Please take your time to read these scriptures for yourself. Let them get down in your heart and work in you. Look these up in the version that you like to read, like the Message or Amplified version.

Unless otherwise noted, these scriptures are found in the New Living Translation. King James Version will be noted with KJV.

Genesis
1:26–27, 22:13–14
Numbers
14:17–18, 18:29, 23:19
Deuteronomy
6:5, 11:13–14, 30:16, 31:6, 33:27
Joshua
1:9, 2:11, 24:15
1 Samuel
15:29
2 Samuel
22:2, 22:33
1 Chronicles
16:11
2 Chronicles
16:9, 20:17

Psalms (Most of this book, look them up in NLT and KJV)
1:3, 3:3, 4:3, 4:5, 4:8, 5:3, 5:11–12, 9:1–2, 12:6, 13:6, 16:1/8/11, 17:8, 18:1–2, 19:14, 20:5, 21:2/6, 23:1–6, 24:8/10, 25:1–25, 27:1–14, 30:1–2/5/10–12, 31:3/14/24, 32:1–11, 33:20–22, 34:1/2/4/8/13–14/18–22 (KJV), 35:27–28, 36:4–7/9, 37:1–40, 38:22, 39:1–13, 40:2/33, 40:5/16, 41:11, 41:8–9, 42:1/7, 43:5, 44:21, 46:1–11, 47:1, 48:14, 50:6, 50:14–15, 50:23, 51:1–19, 54:1–7, 55:1–3/16–19, 55:22–23, 56:3–4/9–13, 57:1–3/7, 58:9–10, 59:9/16–17, 61:1–4, 62:1–2/5–8/11, 63:1–11, 64:10, 65:11–13, 66:8–12/16–20, 67:1, 68:3–4/6/9–11/19/35, 69:13–18/30–36, 70:1–5, 71:1–6/15–18/21–24, 72:13/17–19, 73:23–28, 74:12, 75:6–10, 77:1–3/12–15/20, 78:7, 80:3, 82:6, 83:18, 84:11, 85:12, 90:17, 91:1–2, 91:11–12, 94:19, 96:1–13, 97:10–12, 98:3, 100:4–5, 103:8–12, 111:3, 115:11, 117:2, 118:6–9, 118:24, 119:105, 119:172, 130:7, 138, 139:14, 149:4
Proverbs
3:5–7, 3:11–18, 8:19, 9:6, 9:10, 10:31, 11:14 (KJV), 12:15, 15:2, 15:31, 18:10, 18:21, 18:24, 20:12, 21:21, 31:8–9
Ecclesiastes
3:1–22
Isaiah
1:8, 7:9, 12:2–3, 14:10, 14:27, 26:3–4, 29:16, 30:15, 32:17, 37:20, 40:31, 41:10, 43:1, 43:19, 44:10, 45:2, 45:8, 46:11, 54:14, 54:17, 55:9, 60:22, 61:1–11, 64:8, 65:1–2
Jeremiah
1:4–5, 17:7, 18:6, 29:11–14, 31:14
Lamentations
3:1–66
Daniel
3:1–30, 6:1–24
Micah
5:4 (KJV), 7:8 (NASB)
Habakkuk
2:1–3, 3:18
Zechariah
2:8–9 (KJV), 13:9

Matthew
5:14, 5:16, 5:44, 6:1–34, 7:7, 7:11, 7:24–27, 11:28–30, 12:21, 12:22–37, 14:27, 16:13–20, 17:20, 18:15–20, 19:26, 21:21–22, 22:14, 22:37–39, 25:1–46, 26:39

Mark
2:22, 9:23–24, 11:23, 12:41–44, 16:17

Luke
1:37, 4:18, 6:28, 6:37–38, 12:48, 21:1–4, 24:49

John
3:12 NKJV, 3:16–18, 3:30, 4:1–42, 5:4, 6:29, 7:38, 8:32, 8:36, 8:44, 10:10, 14:1, 14:10, 14:16, 14:23, 14:26–29, 15:4, 15:15, 15:18, 16:5–15, 16:16–33, 19:30

Acts
2:21, 5:31, 10:4, 10:9–11, 10:13, 10:43, 11:6, 11:22, 11:24, 11:29–36, 12:6–8, 12:11–21, 14:22–23, 16:31, 20:5, 20:22–24, 20:35, 26;16, 27:25

Romans
1:7, 1:16, 3:24, 5:1–2, 5:8, 5:16–21, 6:18, 8:1–39, 9:21, 11:6, 11:17, 11:29, 11:31, 12:1–2, 12:8–10, 12:12, 12:21, 15:4

1 Corinthians
1:3, 1:27, 1:30, 2:9, 10:13, 12:4–11, 13:1–13, 16:14, 16:18, 16:23

2 Corinthians
1:3–4, 3:1–6, 3:16–18, 4:16, 5:1–26, 6:2, 6:4, 6:18, 7:1, 9:13–15

Galatians
1:3, 2:16, 3:26, 4:7, 4:17, 5:1–26, 6:3, 6:6–10, 6:14–15

Ephesians
1:2–23, 2:3–10, 2:13–22, 3:6–12, 3:16–21, 4:1–16, 4:20–24, 4:29–32, 5:1–2, 5:15–16, 5:29, 6:6–7, 6:10–18, 6:23–24

Philippians
1:6, 1:20, 2:9–11, 3:13–15 KJV, 4:6–7, 4:13, 4:23

Colossians
1:6, 1:9–29, 2:2–23, 3:1–25, 4:2–6

1 Thessalonians
3:8, 5:1–28

2 Thessalonians
3:3, 3:5

1 Timothy
1:14
2 Timothy
1:6–11, 1:14, 2:1, 2:3–4, 2:7, 2:24–26, 3:12, 3:16–17, 4:1–2, 4:18
Titus
2:14
Hebrews
1:1–14, 2:1–4, 2:10–15, 2:18, 4:12, 8:12 (KJV), 9:15, 9:28, 10:36, 11:1, 11:6, 12:1–2, 13:1–2, 13:8–9, 13:15–16, 13:25
James
1:2–4, 1:5–6, 1:12, 1:17, 2:13, 3:1–18, 4:1–17, 5:1–20
1 Peter
1:2, 1:7, 1:19, 2:9–10, 4:8, 5:8, 5:10–11
2 Peter
1:1–25, 2:1–25, 3:1–22 KJV
1 John
1:7–9, 2:4, 2:15, 2:27–29, 3:1, 3:16, 3:24, 4:1–21, 5:1, 5:4, 5:18–20
3 John
1:3
Revelation
1:8, 3:20 (KJV), 12:11, 19:16, 21:6

CITATIONS

"Love means never having to say you're sorry" (Erich Segal, *Love Story*).

Pastor Robert Morris from Gateway Church. Sermon series called *Free Indeed*. Sermon quoted "Open Gates, Set Free."

"Jesus still loved you and picked you when your past was still your future. Let me say it again. When your history was still your future, God loved you" (My pastor, Pastor Ron Carpenter Jr.)

"I deliberately carve out time in my prayer life to be still and listen for God's voice" (Priscilla Shirer, *Discerning the Voice of God. How to Recognize When God Is Speaking*).

Webster's dictionary.

The Bible for all the scriptures.

"No matter what you are going through, someone else has faced it with Jesus and was victorious on the other side" (Pastor Ron Carpenter Jr).

"The purpose of the voice of condemnation is to push you away from his presence-that which is the very source of your victory. The purpose of the voice of conviction is to press you into the face of Christ" (Bob Sorge in Priscilla Shirer's *Discerning the Voice of God*).

"The same Good News that came to you is going out all over the world. It is changing lives everywhere, just as it changed yours that very first day you heard and understood the truth about God's great kindness to sinners." Colossians 1:6 NLT

ABOUT THE AUTHOR

Sara was born and raised in Kansas City and currently resides in Central Texas. She loves Jesus, her family, friends, and her dog. She loves to cook and experiment with new recipes. She really enjoys long car rides with in-car karaoke. Sara has always marched to her very own beat.

CPSIA information can be obtained
at www.ICGtesting.com
Printed in the USA
LVHW022025151121
703363LV00002B/169